The Art of Nietzsche

Colophon

ISBN: 9789051798654

Published in 2014 by
Gopher B.V.
Keizersgracht 75-II
1015 CE Amsterdam
The Netherlands

Design book cover: based on a painting 'Points of Light Moving on the Square' by Anders Lidén
Design title pages: Lisette Huizenga
Visual Art: Martin Sjardijn, Ditty Ketting, Lisette Huizenga, Suzanne Bo, Lichel van den Ende, Sydney Sitters
Photography: Jan van Zelderen, Arnold Cocu

This publication was made possible thanks to financial support from:
The Prins Bernard Culture Foundation
Foundation 'Stroom'
Pulchri Studio

This book comes with recordings of compositions by Nietzsche and settings of his poetry by Mahler, Delius, Orff, Webern, Rihm and Woodward.
©Foundation TransMusings.
Website: http://transmusings.org/home/The_Art_of_Nietzsche_Music.html

The Art of Nietzsche

Anne Borsboom
Piet Steenbakkers
Anne Woodward

UITGEVERIJ gopher
www.gopher.nl

Contents

Introduction **8**
- Anne Woodward

Nietzsche 'understood' as an artist **10**
How artists 'understood' Nietzsche **30**
- Anne Woodward

Conversations with artists **36**
Lisette Huizenga 38
Lichel van den Ende 45
Suzanne Bo 50
Ditty Ketting 54
- Anne Borsboom
- Translation: Francine van Sambeek and Kerry Woodward

Why Nietzsche wrote such good music **58**
- Piet Steenbakkers

A journey **70**
Martin Sjardijn 72
Kerry Woodward 76
- Anne Borsboom
- Translation: Francine van Sambeek and Kerry Woodward

Reflections **83**
- Anne Borsboom and Anne Woodward
- Translation: Kerry Woodward

The Music **86**

Song texts **88**
- Translations: Kerry Woodward

The Word

The living word is my companion:
Who jumps up at me so cheerfully,
And greets me with a friendly nod,
Lovely even in its awkwardness,
Full-blooded, snorting heartily,
Even crawling into deaf ears,
Entwining itself and now fluttering,
And whatever it does - the word delights.
Even so, the word remains a tender being,
Soon sick, though quickly cured.
To let it have its little life,
Hold it light and delicate,
Don't touch or squeeze it roughly,
Often it will die just from evil glances –
And lies there then, so deformed,
So soulless, poor and cold,
Its tiny corpse wickedly transformed,
Abused by death and dying.
A dead word – a hideous thing,
A bone-dry rattling kling-kling-kling.
Yuck to all those hateful trades,
Wherein word and words expire!

Nietzsche

Introduction

The guiding motive behind 'The Art of Nietzsche' is Nietzsche's own passionate desire to be appreciated and understood as an artist. In preparation for this book, we presented several concerts and a visual art exhibition at Pulchri Studio in The Hague. Through these events, and especially through this book with its particular music recordings, we have placed Nietzsche under the spotlight as a poet and composer, while exploring how some of his philosophical thoughts relate not only to his own art but to art and artists of today. We were intrigued by the very existence of Nietzsche's music. Most of his pieces are rarely performed, and then often badly, so we wondered if his music deserved a wider and better advocacy. Also we wanted to discover if approaching Nietzsche as an artist might shed new light on his philosophy, so often qualified as 'difficult' or 'obscure'. This book and the music recordings illustrate that the answer to both these questions is in the affirmative. By looking at Nietzsche's work through an artist's eyes, not only at his poetry and music but also at some of his philosophical ideas, justice is done to his urgent call to study him from this perspective and not from that of the spectator.

Thus, the thread running through the chapters of this book, however different and personal they may appear to be, is a response to Nietzsche's wish. All the visual artists, musicians and writers involved discovered that this approach proved fruitful, bringing musical pleasure, poetic beauty, inspiration and a clearer understanding of Nietzsche's philosophical thoughts, as well as an enthusiasm to look at emerging and new artistic visions.

This approach to Nietzsche's work is enhanced by the diversity of the three writers, their styles and subjects:

Anne Woodward,
musician and philosopher, explores what it means to understand Nietzsche's ideas from 'the perspective of the artist' and why Nietzsche has been such a source of inspiration for many composers and visual artists, past and present.

Anne Borsboom,
poet and writer, talks with five visual artists and a composer, all involved in creating visual works and music based on Nietzsche's thoughts and poetry, about their experiences and the inspiration Nietzsche provided. She interweaves her own impressions and ponderings throughout these interviews.

Piet Steenbakkers,
lecturer in the history of modern philosophy at the University of Utrecht and holder of the Chair of Spinoza Studies at the Erasmus University, Rotterdam, argues that a chapter entitled, *Why I write such good music*, would not have been amiss in Nietzsche's autobiography, *Ecce homo*. Piet discusses the merits of Nietzsche's music and poetry in relation to Nietzsche's philosophy.

The musical recordings, containing compositions by Gustav Mahler, Frederick Delius, Carl Orff, Wolfgang Rihm, Kerry Woodward and Friedrich Nietzsche himself, are grouped around four themes:

No
- everything that Nietzsche denies and rejects

Only fool, only poet!
- Nietzsche's own compositions

Wandering
- his lonely search for meaning

Yes
- his *amor fati* (love of fate) and unconditional affirmation of life.

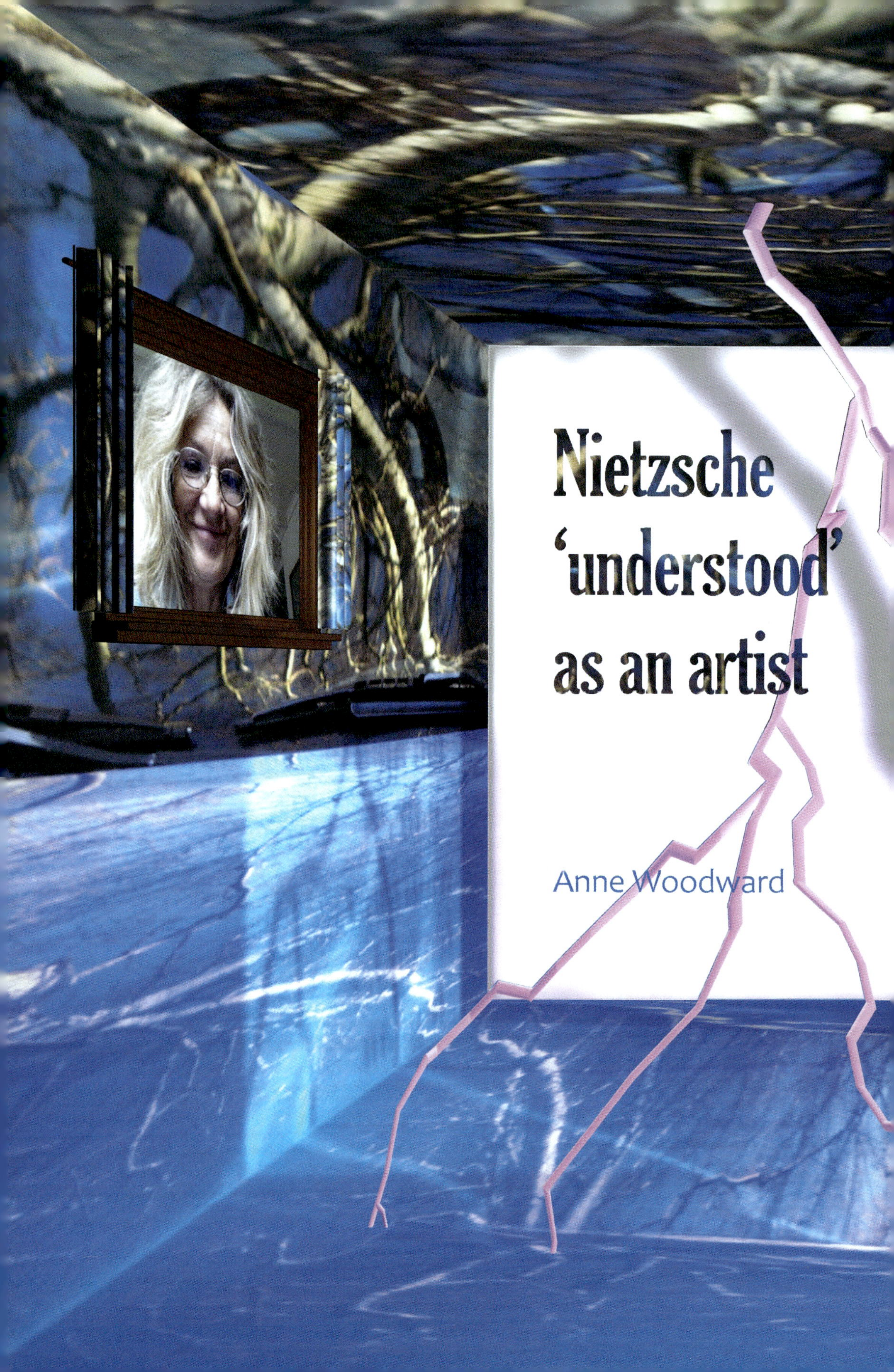
Nietzsche
'understood'
as an artist
Anne Woodward

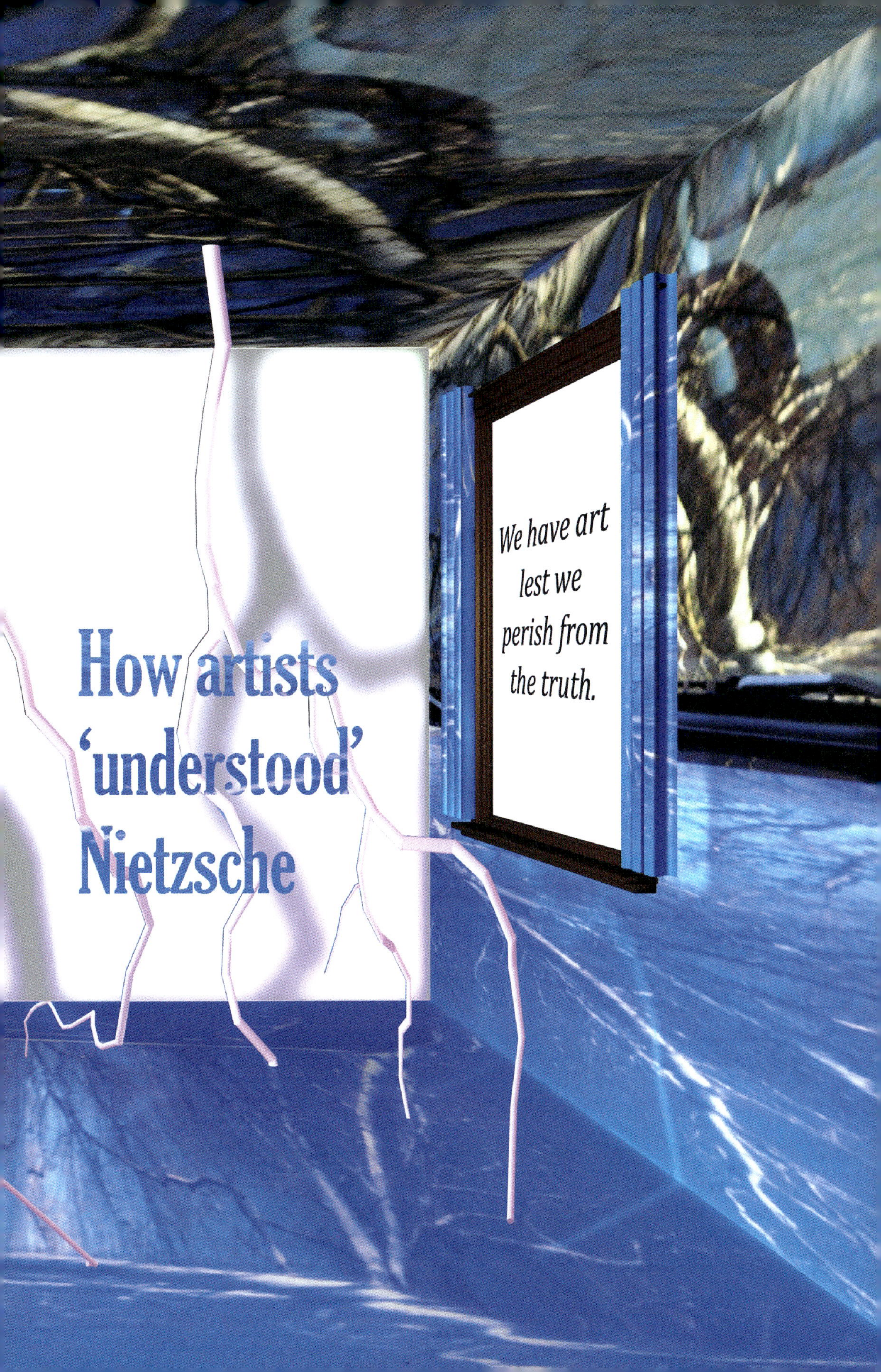
How artists
'understood'
Nietzsche
We have art
lest we
perish from
the truth.

Nietzsche 'understood' as an artist

Ecce homo

Ja! Ich weiß, woher ich stamme!
Ungesättigt gleich der Flamme
glühe und verzehr' ich mich.
Licht wird alles, was ich fasse,
Kohle alles, was ich lasse:
Flamme bin ich sicherlich!

Ecce homo

Yes! I know from whence I come,
Insatiable as the flame
I glow and consume myself.
Everything I grasp becomes light,
Whatever I leave is ashes:
For, assuredly, I am flame!

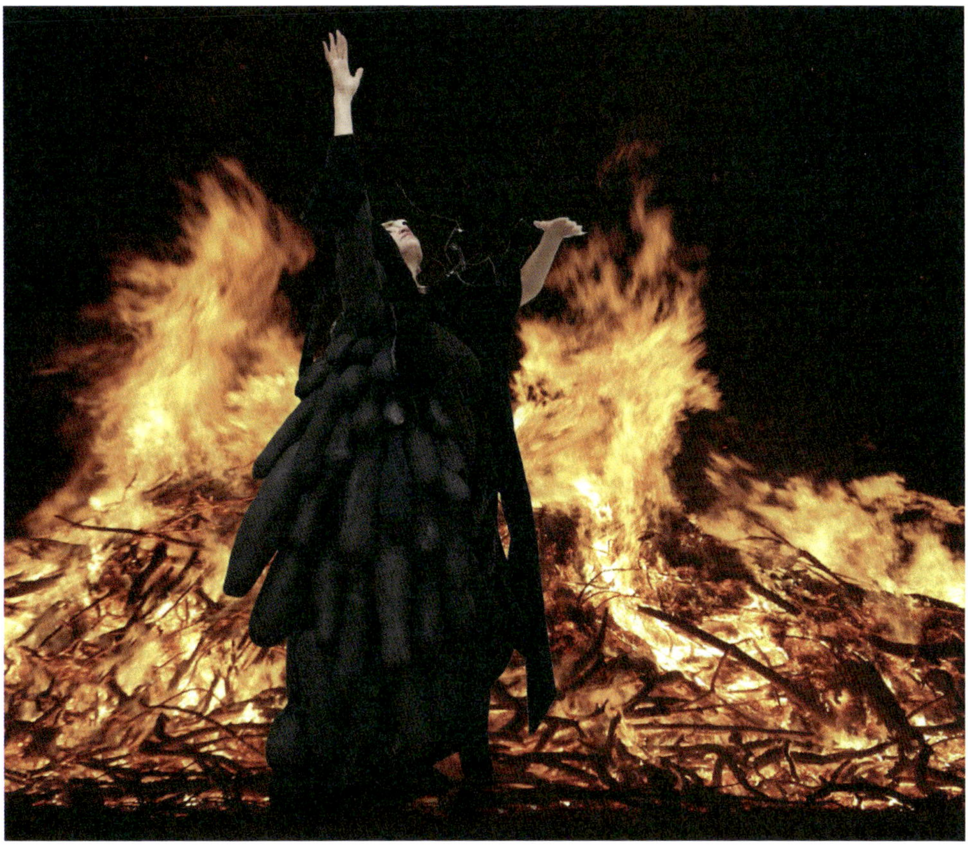

Wearable Art – Lichel van den Ende. Photo: Arnold Cocu

The flame called Friedrich Nietzsche resided in a megalomaniac personality with a radically sceptical mind, a sickly body, overpowering emotions and a deeply religious soul. 'Religious' in the sense of being driven by a 'higher' vision to which he had to give testimony at all costs. His credo, 'let me be banished from all truth', did not prevent him from searching for new insights, time and again, and using himself as guinea pig for the 'experimental philosophy as I live it... I am neither mind nor body, but a *tertium quid*.'[1] A restless seeker, not for an absolute truth - of which he denied the possibility - but for healing and a state of health, of himself, but above all, of our western culture that, in his view, was heading for disaster:

> *Already for centuries, our whole European culture has been moving... towards a catastrophe: restless, violent and rash like a mighty river longing for its ending, no longer contemplating, terrified of reflection... soon, where we live, no one will be able to exist.*[2]

Lou Salomé, the unattainable love of his life, once characterized him as 'a man either in a state of falling ill through thoughts or being cured by thoughts'. His final insanity, most likely caused by syphilis, is described by some as the inescapable result of his philosophical experiments and his cultivated 'high altitude loneliness', and even as fictitious and self-created.

The disparity between the greatness of my assignment and the smallness of my contemporaries is revealed by the fact that people have neither heard nor even seen me,[3] Nietzsche bitterly writes, in *Ecce homo*, his own critique of his complete works, shortly before he slides into a state of permanent insanity. And at the very end of it, he asks three times, as a symbol of the betrayal he foresees: *Have I been understood? Have I been understood? Have I been understood?*

Nietzsche was a poet, a prophet and a visionary writer who wrapped his messages in paradoxes, walking a tightrope between the rational and the intuitive. His work, in prose and poetry, has yielded numerous interpretations and still elicits both veneration and disgust.

With brilliance, and an often graceful though sometimes bombastic style and biting sarcasm, he makes devastating attacks on German idealism, Christianity and conventional moral values; and due to the enormous resistance this evoked, the liberating part of his message often went unnoticed. Many people still shudder at his outrageous attacks on other thinkers, his call for 'hardness' and a 'master morality', and his supposed lack of charity, whereby 'charity' is then often mistaken for 'pity'.

---

1. Lou Salomé, *Nietzsche*, translated and edited by Siegfried Mandel (University of Illinois Press, 2001), p. xxxviii/xxxix.
2. Friedrich Nietzsche, *Sämtliche Werke: Kritische Studienausgabe*, hrsg. von Giorgio Colli und Mazzino Montinari (=KSA), 3. Aufl. (München: Deutscher Taschenbuch Verlag, 1999), Band 13, p.189. Translation: Anne Woodward.
3. *Ecce homo - Vorwort* (KSA 6, 257).

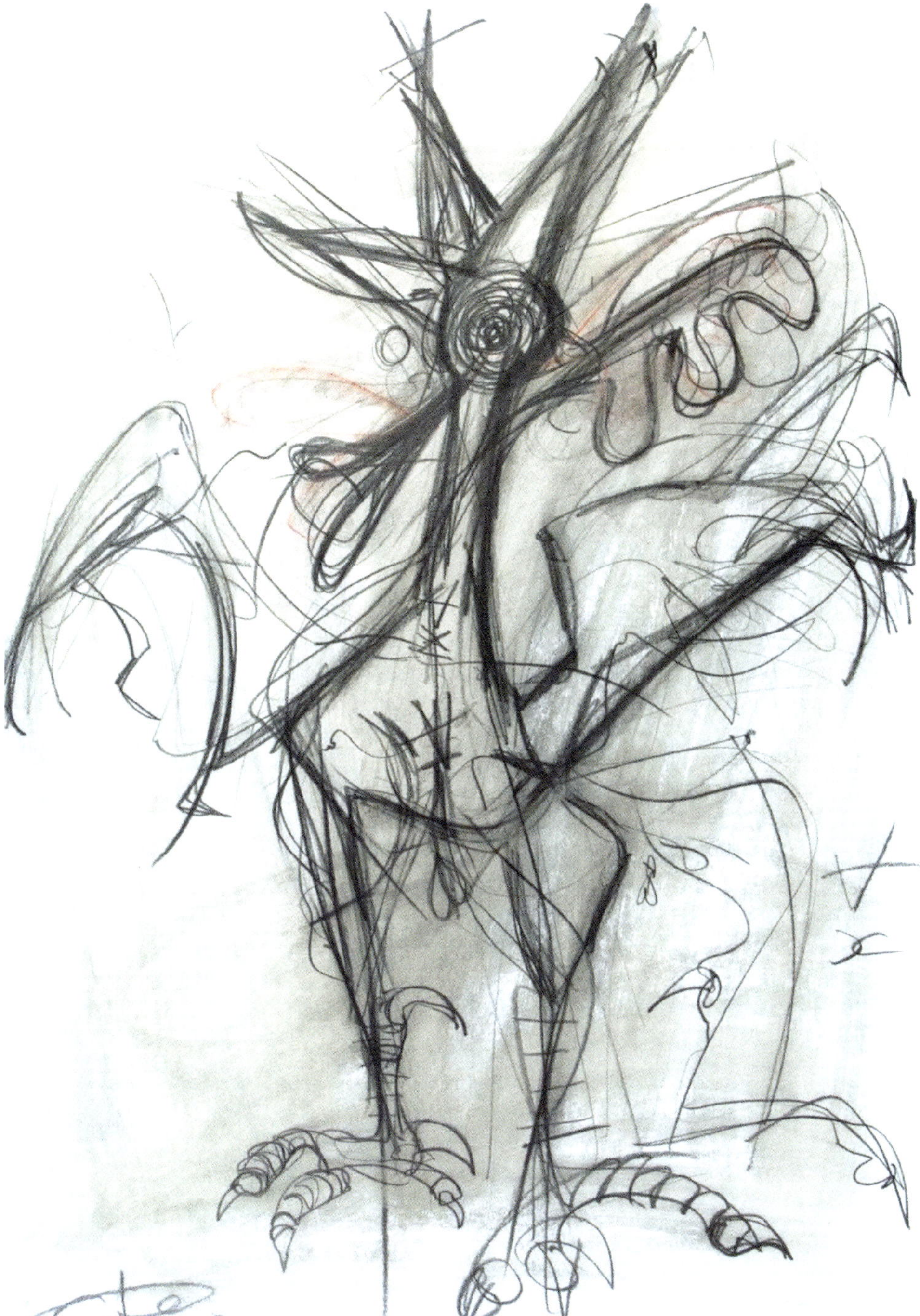

Cock - Sydney Sitters

Nietzsche did not expect otherwise:

> *Our deepest insights must — and should — sound as follies, and under certain circumstances, as crimes, when, in an unauthorized way, they reach the ears of those not disposed and ordained to hear them.*[1]

He wants his statements to be understood 'esoterically' and not 'exoterically', where the essential distinction between these perspectives is:

> *that the exoteric views things from below upwards — while the esoteric views things FROM ABOVE DOWNWARDS. There are heights of the soul from which tragedy itself no longer appears to operate tragically.*[2]

Nietzsche's premonition that he would be misunderstood certainly came true; the misuses that the National Socialists made of his ideas, such as the 'will to power' (interpreted as a nationalistic incentive) and the 'Übermensch' (as a representative of the superior Aryan race), are sad examples.

An association with anti-Semitism and fascism has long clouded his work; this was due largely to his sister Elisabeth, who, after Nietzsche's death, turned down the offer of his loyal friend, Peter Gast, to edit the numerous, unpublished manuscripts. She took on this task personally and, with no scruples about blatant deception and counterfeiting, she integrated her anti-Semitic ideas into Nietzsche's texts and created an impression of closeness between her brother and herself. These forgeries have been uncovered only gradually, the full scale of her deceit emerged much later. Ironically, her anti-Semitism and Christian fundamentalism, and her continuous attempts to dominate Nietzsche were the explicit reasons for him breaking off all relationship with her.

The breach with his initial idol, Richard Wagner, was also due partly to the anti-Semitism of the latter, as well as to Wagner's supposed relapse into Christian morality, although the 'deadly mode' of Wagner's 'insult' was undoubtedly crucial as well. Wagner had indeed committed an unforgivable indiscretion by openly discussing with Nietzsche's physician 'the deterioration of Nietzsche's eyesight due to frequent masturbation', a story that consequently did the full round during the opening of the 1882 Bayreuth Festival.

---

1. *Jenseits von Gut und Böse* (KSA 5, 49).
2. *Jenseits von Gut und Böse* (KSA 5, 49).

Later, in his pamphlet *Nietzsche contra Wagner* Nietzsche wrote:

> *By the summer of 1876, during the time of the first Festival, I said farewell to Wagner in my heart... step by step, he had condescended to everything I despise — even to anti-Semitism... It was high time indeed to say farewell: soon after, I received the proof. Richard Wagner — seemingly utterly triumphant, but in truth, a mellowed, beaten and desperate decadent — suddenly sank down, helpless and broken, before the Christian cross.*[1]

Still, even after Nietzsche's resurrection in the 1970s and the growing acceptance and enthusiasm for his work, the problem remains that he simply put out so many ideas without explanation, and often seemed to contradict himself. Despite Bärenreiter's publication of his complete musical compositions in 1985 (a real labour of love by Curt Paul Janz), their existence and merit are still little known. And, though his impact on twentieth century art is generally recognised, it is far from clear which particular elements were the source of inspiration for so many great writers, poets, visual artists and composers. It is often assumed that such geniuses as Mahler, Strauss and Picasso just responded emotionally to Nietzsche's ideas without having properly understood his philosophy.

However, almost immediately after his mental collapse, in the world of art, themes such as 'the Dionysian', 'the Superman' and 'the eternal recurrence' were found to be rich sources of inspiration. In fact, *Thus spoke Zarathustra* has become the most frequently musically portrayed philosophical work of all times. Artists understood him better, and definitely earlier, than philosophers. This is hardly surprising, since Nietzsche himself was an artist. His work, which he himself considers for the most part to be art, can, in his view, only be understood from the perspective of the artist and not from that of the spectator. With *Thus spoke Zarathustra* he even attempted to wrap his philosophy completely in an artistic form, trusting in the intuitive transmission of philosophical insights through images and poetical language.

Nietzsche's philosophy is born out of passion, first of all, for music: *without music life for me would be a mistake*;[2] for friendship, initially with Wagner; and later, for ever higher 'visions' - direct insights into reality - which, however, can never reveal a permanent truth. He had already realised this at a very early age, writing in his diary: *Even the highest truth can only be a symbol for an even higher truth.*

Whoever reads Nietzsche only to get to know his rational explanations of reality or to judge how right or wrong he was, will be left empty-handed. The reader must be willing to adopt the perspective of the artist and search in the higher regions of his soul.

---

1. *Nietzsche contra Wagner* (KSA 6, 431). It must be said that this attack seems somewhat hypocritical. In the beginning of his friendship with Wagner, most likely in order to impress him, but particularly Wagner's wife, Cosima, Nietzsche had written an article that certainly did contain anti-Semitic elements. But from numerous later statements about this subject it is clear that it was Jewish culture (as well as Christian and most of all, German) that he opposed, and absolutely not the Jewish race.
2. *Nietzsche to Brandes,* 27 March 1888, letter 1009.

But what does this mean?

Nietzsche was convinced that human life cannot be explained by theoretical speculations, but can only be approached conceptually with dream-images, with works of art, with descriptions of emotional and intuitive experiences and with apparently paradoxical statements. He does not seek to convince us with arguments or proofs, but rather with intuitive or 'artistic' insights intended to kindle our own intuitive powers. This is just how a painter or composer attempts to communicate, consciously or subconsciously. Being open to intuitive impressions in image, sound or language and being aware of one's intuitive reactions to these, and only perhaps secondarily wanting to explain them, is the perspective of the artist. The question then becomes not: was Nietzsche right, but: has he succeeded in communicating his visions so that they spark off new insights in us?

This does not mean that we should reject or numb our rational powers. Rather, the rational mind must function as a razor-sharp dissecting knife in order to explore all those ideas that come in the wake of a 'higher' vision. The Dionysian state is a creative trance where the mind is fully awake. Although, in 'The Birth of Tragedy', Nietzsche did not deny that it would be possible to enter the Dionysian through the use of drugs or rituals, in his later works, he never suggests suppressing or ignoring the rational mind or cultivating an irrational expression of emotions. On the contrary, Nietzsche considers emotions and personal feelings as being often mere echoes of out-dated moral principles:

> *To trust one's feelings, that means, obeying one's grandfather and grandmother and their grandparents instead of obeying the gods, who are inside US: our reason and our experience.*[1]

To create, we must evoke all our powers: not by a leap of faith over the rational, but by seeking ever-higher perspectives of the mind.

Concerning the artistic and philosophical processes of creating, he writes:

> *One hears, one does not seek; one takes, one does not ask who gives: suddenly, like lightning, a thought flashes up, out of necessity, without faltering — I have never had a choice... Everything happens completely involuntarily, as in a tempestuous surge of freedom, of absoluteness, of power, of divinity…*[2]

And:

> *Being born and passing away, constructing and destroying, without any moral liability, in everlasting innocence, that is only possible, in this world, in the play of the artist and the child. And thus, just like the child and the artist, the eternal, living fire plays, creates and destroys — in total innocence…*[3]

---

1. *Morgenröte* (KSA 3, 44).
2. *Ecce homo - Also sprach Zarathustra* (KSA 6, 339).
3. *Die Philosophie im tragischen Zeitalter der Griechen* (KSA 1, 830).

Nietzsche is often criticised for his inconsistency and lack of systematisation. His position, however, is that the desire for a system springs from a lack of integrity, and that rigidity of judgments can lead only to ruin: *The snake that cannot shed its skin, must die. The same is valid for the mind that cannot change its opinions; it ceases to be a mind.*[1]

Nietzsche does not aim at moulding reality into a philosophical model of coherent truths. Quite the contrary, he sees that his specific task is to destroy all crystallised ideas, ideals and idols, including his own. There are no truths or facts, only interpretations. By reducing certainties, prejudices and principles to ashes, he makes room for new 'truths', which he has to destroy over and over again, because there is no final goal, no ideal and no resting place. *Overthrowing idols, (my word for "ideals")... is part of my craft.*[2]

In this context, we should also consider the mysterious advice that Zarathustra gives to his 'disciples':

> *Verily, I advise you: depart from me, and guard yourselves against Zarathustra! And better still: be ashamed of him! Perhaps he hath deceived you.*[3]

Zarathustra tells his followers not to 'believe' in him, convinced that every form of fundamentalism and every cherished truth will annihilate our chances of freedom and creativity. Only on the solitary heights of thinking and experiencing without prejudice will it be possible to change perspectives, to choose and truly create. We have to climb such a mountain ourselves!

Therefore: no systems, no dogmas and no faith in anything at all. Nevertheless, we can discover clear and consequent lines of thought in Nietzsche's philosophy, which could compare with the 'Leitmotiv' found in the music of, for example, Wagner, Berlioz and Strauss. Through its recurrences and transformations a leitmotif provides coherence in extensive compositions, such as the four operas constituting Wagner's *The Ring of the Nibelung*. It is a short, recognisable musical theme that symbolises a person, an idea or an object; it is developed gradually and appears in different forms and colours and sometimes even as a reversal of itself. We could say that in Nietzsche's work a number of these leitmotifs are present, such as the 'Dionysian', the meaning of art and the liberation from all illusion.

---

1. *Morgenröte* (KSA 3, 330).
2. *Ecce homo - Vorwort* (KSA 6, 258).
3. *Also sprach Zarathustra* (KSA 4, 101).

The Dionysian

Still heavily under the influence of Schopenhauer, Nietzsche writes his first important work: *The Birth of Tragedy out of the Spirit of Music*, as a flaming pamphlet in defence of the 'Gesamtkunstwerk' of Richard Wagner. Nietzsche depicts him as a saviour of western culture, naturally to the delight of Wagner himself, in whose operas, according to Nietzsche, the Dionysian and the Apollonian are in a perfect and healing balance, just as in ancient Greek tragedy. The Dionysian represents the primal power of being, our intuitive knowledge of the unity of all things and the joy of being at one with the whole of nature. The Apollonian, on the other hand, represents our dream world, where we experience ourselves as separated individuals, striving for order and beauty.

Man has, and essentially is, the will to eternal life; yet, dreaming of peace and harmony, he finds himself destined for struggle, pain and death. With all his ideals of purpose, beauty and happiness, he is the prisoner of an all powerful, but completely aimless and disinterested nature. From this tragedy, art is born and only she can reconcile man with his fate.

> *Then... that saviour sorceress, expert in healing, Art, approaches; only she can turn the nausea of the horror and absurdity of life into imaginations with which it is possible to live: these are the sublime art that constrains our terror, and the comic that releases us from our loathing of the absurdity.*[1]

In the original Greek tragedies of Sophocles and Aeschylus, the essence of our life is made visible and audible through the combination of the music and the chorus (the Dionysian), and the actors and the narrative poetry (the Apollonian). The performance gives us the opportunity to feel at one with the primal power of being and, from that perspective, to witness the suffering and savagery of human life. This experience makes our suffering tolerable, because all pain is caused by individuation and separation, and the spectacle allows us to 'enjoy' our misery and death by watching it from the Dionysian perspective of primordial unity.
But alas, Greek tragedy and thereby the relief of man's tragic fate, died at the hands of the poet Euripides and the evil spirit behind him: Socrates, the first philosopher who believed that we could know and control the depths of life and our emotions simply by applying the principles of logic and causality. Euripides removed the chorus from his tragedies and introduced a purely Apollonian spectacle, in which we now had to see the story from a moral perspective.
For example, the tragedy 'The Bacchantes' demonstrates how dangerous a submission to Dionysus can be: during a Dionysian orgy, a whole town is destroyed and a son torn to pieces by his own mother.

Nietzsche points out that the Apollonian, when separated from its Dionysian foundation, will ultimately destroy any culture because it cuts itself off from all life force, under the illusion that pure reason is able to control nature and sweep the horrifying aspects of life under the carpet, without reprisal. But the Dionysian is life itself, always re-emerging unexpectedly and violently, while the Apollonian

1. *Die Geburt der Trägodie* (KSA 1, 57).

man can only be a doomed shadow of himself. According to Nietzsche, the 'Enlightenment' began with Socrates but is now as dead as mutton.

The Dionysian plays a crucial role in Nietzsche's philosophy and he develops this idea throughout his whole oeuvre. As we have seen, initially, he contrasts the Dionysian with the Apollonian, but later the Apollonian is wholly incorporated into the Dionysian where it then represents a higher vision or intuition. Now, 'vital' art is born out of the overflowing life force, the unlimited energy of 'becoming', which must be viewed from a higher perspective in order to embrace it joyfully. Nietzsche now juxtaposes the Dionysian with the romantic and decadent, that is, the art of the depressed, despairing individual who complains about his inability to attain his ideals, because he does not realise the necessity of everything, exactly as it manifests itself. But with the Dionysian, we embrace our fate with love, with an *amor fati*. This means to assert an unconditional 'yes' to life, with a simultaneous and passionate 'no' to everything that denies life and is concerned with illusions, which, in Nietzsche's view, includes all metaphysical and religious truths.

Finally, he comes to the conclusion that Dionysian art is not only a stimulus to life, but is life itself. It is this art that wants to convince us incessantly of the eternal joys of being and of the psychological state that comes with it: the will to experience, to exalt, to confirm one's inherent power, to create from an overabundance of love and vitality, while suffering is just the pain of labour accompanying the unending birth of new truths and joy.

Might Nietzsche have found inspiration here in the ideas of Spinoza? Many people, not least Nietzsche himself, have pointed out the similarities between the two philosophers. Thus Nietzsche, caught in his accustomed 'illusion' of complete loneliness, writes to his friend Franz Overbeck:

> *I am utterly amazed, utterly enchanted! I have a precursor, and what a precursor! I hardly knew Spinoza: that I longed to read him just now, was an "instinctual act."... this most unusual and loneliest thinker is closest to me precisely in these matters: he denies the freedom of the will, teleology, the moral world-order, the unegoistic, evil... In summa: my loneliness, which, as on very high mountains, often made it hard for me to breathe... is now at least a twosomeness.*[1]

Spinoza teaches that the highest form of knowledge, which he calls the *scientia intuitiva*, gives us the key to the acceptance of all aspects of life, to inner peace and to beatitude. But this intuitive knowledge is only possible when founded upon reason as well as upon the knowledge of experience. Intuitive knowledge is the immediate understanding of singular things from the perspective of eternity or, we could say, is the intuitive understanding of all things as eternal. This form of knowledge shows us the necessity of everything, just as it is and as it happens, while simultaneously generating extreme joy and love. Nietzsche's description of his viewing things from great heights, of his concept of the eternal recurrence

1. Sils-Maria, July 30, 1881: Postcard to Franz Overbeck.

that gives equal importance and eternity to each moment, and of his *amor fati*, the confirmation of the necessity of every single aspect of life, seems quite close to some of Spinoza's ideas. It is quite untrue that, in emphasising the importance of higher and intuitive visions in his later work, Nietzsche rejected the rational and scientific thinking of his so-called positivistic period, or that he became metaphysical or even purely mystical, as some commentators have claimed. He did indeed climb ever higher up the mountain. For, though rational knowledge is not the highest form of knowledge, it is a necessary step in acquiring any higher knowledge. Intuition, paired with joy and an unconditional love of life, must be based on instinct, but also on reason: this form of intuition is, ultimately, the Dionysian perspective. When Nietzsche speaks of higher perspectives or visions, it can be helpful to consider Spinoza's concept of the *scientia intuitiva*.

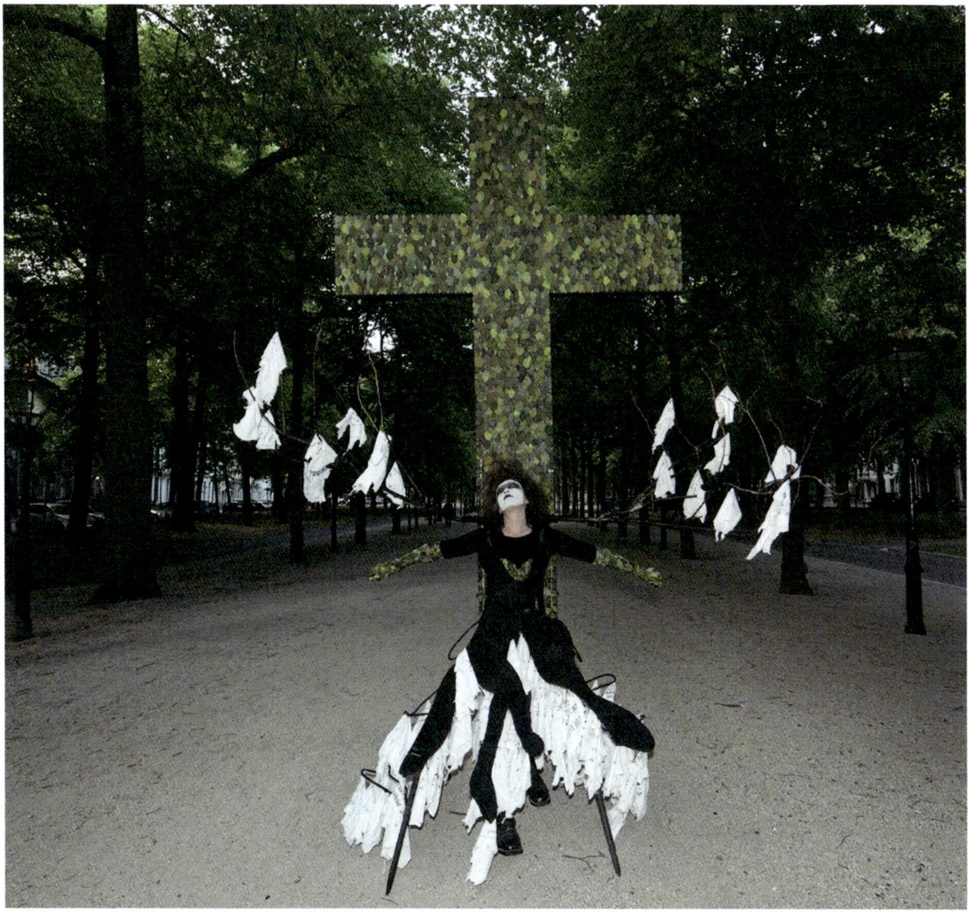

Nietzsche-parade on the avenue 'Lange Voorhout' in The Hague – Lichel van den Ende. Photo: Arnold Cocu

The Death of God

The most devastating and still echoing thunderbolt that Nietzsche hurled into the world is, of course: *God is dead… and we, you and I, have killed him…*[1]

On the one hand, the death of God is an unprecedented catastrophe, with life threatening consequences, on the other hand, it provides us with a breath-taking perspective of a new freedom:

… that "the old God" is dead... thereby our heart flows over with gratitude, amazement, awe, expectation — finally the free horizon reappears... finally our ships can set sail again... every venture to acquire knowledge is permitted again... our sea lies open once more... perhaps we have never had such an open sea.[2]

And, in contrast:

> *God is dead! God remains dead! And we have killed him! How can we comfort ourselves, murderers of all murderers? The holiest and mightiest that the world has ever possessed, bled to death under our knives: who will wipe this blood off us?... Is not the greatness of this deed too great for us? Must we not become gods ourselves, just to appear worthy of this deed?*[3]

God's death robs everything of its value and meaning and gives free reign to 'nihilism'. A nihilist sees the world in which we live as a meaningless reality that should not be, while the world as it should be can never exist.
But God remains dead. Clinging on to the certainties of an out-dated religion, which is now, literally, 'unbelievable' and therefore cannot be lived, also means nihilism, and leads to our demise because it denies and suffocates all life force. That God is dead and we have killed him, is a fact that Nietzsche observes everywhere. People do not live and confess their faith at all:

> *The ever more sluggish and instinct-lacking... German people, who with an enviable appetite... without any digestive problems, manage to swallow simultaneously... religion and science, Christian charity and anti-Semitism...*[4]

When Zarathustra delivers this message, it is already long ago that we killed God, but the grim fact has not yet penetrated the consciousness of the people he addresses. Prophetically, he calls on us to admit courageously that we are now free and that it is our own task to give meaning to our lives. The death of God has tremendous consequences because our life is suddenly utterly meaningless and we find ourselves in 'the unbearable lightness of being' as Milan Kundera

---

1. *Die fröhliche Wissenschaft* - 125 (KSA 3, 481).
2. *Die fröhliche Wissenschaft* - 343 (KSA 3, 574). This idea is reflected in the poem *Nach neuen Meeren,* set to music by Frederick Delius and to be heard on the music recordings, no 20.
3. *Die fröhliche Wissenschaft* - 125 (KSA 3, 481).
4. *Ecce homo - der Fall Wagner* (KSA 6, 357/358).

formulated it. Not only is God dead, but all ideas about a metaphysical reality or an organising intelligence behind appearances are illusory. Now, finally, human freedom and the 'overcoming' of man in the direction of the Superman become possible.

Throughout his whole life Nietzsche keeps struggling with the death of God and attempts to recreate all religious values, such as eternal life, beatitude and the ultimate divinity of man, within our earthly reality, instead of in an illusory hereafter. From this struggle his concepts of the 'eternal recurrence' and the 'Superman' are born.

The Eternal Recurrence

A few days after discovering Spinoza, Nietzsche writes:

> *What if, one day or night, a demon were to creep into your loneliest loneliness, and say: "This life, as you now live and have lived it, must be lived by you once again and innumerable times more; and there will be nothing new in it, but every pain and joy and thought and sigh and all the unspeakable greatness and smallness of your life must come again to you, and all in the same sequence — likewise this spider and the moonlight between the trees and also this very moment and I myself. The eternal hourglass of being, will be turned again and again - and you with it, speck of dust!" Would you not throw yourself down and gnash your teeth and curse the demon that thus spoke? Or have you already experienced the awesome moment in which you would have answered: "You are a God and never have I heard anything more divine!" If this thought would overpower you, just as you are now, it might transform or perhaps destroy you; the question concerning all and everybody: "do you want this again and innumerable times more?" would place the heaviest weight on all your actions! How otherwise could you reconcile yourself with yourself and your life than by desiring nothing else than this ultimate, eternal confirmation and sealing?*[1]

This concept of eternity, apart from being derived from the writings of Heraclites and the Stoics, seems to have been inspired by Spinoza, who places the utmost importance on the recognition of the necessity of all things and events and their eternity in the mind of God. As a cosmological, psychological or physical theory, this is obviously an untenable position, and Nietzsche does not seriously attempt to develop it any further. It seems to be a creative leap into the intuitive and esoteric and the best 'truth' for developing a new morality, which, for Nietzsche, is a self-legislation. The idea of the eternal recurrence restores the significance of the past, present and future, and gives an equal weight to every moment of our lives. The Christian doctrines teach us the value of time in the sense that our sins from the past can be forgiven, we can be reborn in the present and can look forward to an eternal future in Heaven (or Hell). Within Nietszche's concept of eternity, the past becomes important again because it has formed us into what we are and know, the present because it provides an opportunity to change our perspectives and morals and the future because it will be a result of those choices. One could say that the eternal recurrence is a moral imperative: only carry out

---

1. *Die fröhliche Wissenschaft* – 341 (KSA 3, 570).

those actions you are willing to repeat for all eternity. And the unconditional and joyful surrender to this is not a submission to total helplessness and fate - that would indeed lead to gnashing of teeth and suicide - but a confirmation of the necessity of the only world there is, ours, and of everything that takes place in it, while our freedom consists in the ability to change perspectives and moral principles. Herein lies our *Lust*, or the eternal joy. Also, we must say an unequivocal 'yes' to our pains and sorrows; they are apparently necessary to purify our views on life. All this requires honesty and the courage to say a radical 'no' to everything that denies our world and our life force.

This new relationship between sorrow and joy is expressed with breath-taking beauty in 'Zarathustra's Midnight Song':

O man, take heed!
What says deep midnight?
"I slept, I slept —,
From deep dreams I have awoken:—
The world is deep,
And deeper than the day had thought.
Deep is its sorrow—,
Joy—deeper still than grief:
Sorrow says: Perish!
But joys all want eternity—,
— want deep, deep eternity!"[1]

The Superman

Another idea, born in the wake of God's death, is that of the superman. In order to be worthy of his murder, we must now become gods ourselves: *God hath died: now do WE desire — the Superman to live.*[2]

Soon after his birth, the 'Superman' became subject of the most outrageous speculations, sometimes resulting in its exact opposite. But Zarathustra spoke: *Never yet hath there been a Superman*[3], and no one can ever be or represent him. Zarathustra himself, often misinterpreted as the first superman, is merely the prophet who announces him; Goethe, Napoleon and other 'heroes', seen also by some as examples of the superman, are, according to Nietzsche, just courageous men who were attempting to realise a higher human potential. The superman is, and remains, an eternal challenge, a goal, whose substance can only be imagined, again and again, because he will always be beyond our comprehension. Man must continually surpass himself, physically and mentally.

---

1. This poem set to music by both Frederick Delius and Gustav Mahler is part of the music recordings (nos. 21 and 22).
2. *Also sprach Zarathustra IV* - (KSA 4, 357).
3. *Also sprach Zarathustra II* - (KSA 4, 119).

I teach you the Superman. All beings hitherto have created something beyond themselves: and ye want to be the ebb of that great tide, and would rather go back to the beast than surpass man?... The Superman is the meaning of the earth. Let your will say: The Superman shall be the meaning of the earth! [1]

An accurate description of this concept has rarely been given,[2] least of all, admittedly, by Nietzsche himself. In contrast with the shameful interpretation of the National Socialists as 'a specimen of the superior Aryan race', we find, contemporaneously, a proper interpretation in the works of Alice A. Bailey:

In Germany, you have the dictatorship of racial superiority, and the attempt to deify a race. Without humour and real understanding, one race is preparing to dictate terms to other races... Yet the idea of a superman is a true ideal, and it needs upholding before the world...[3]

... the only certainty we have is that the doors of the future are wide open... little by little he [man] has grown from the stage of a cave man to that of a Shakespeare, a Newton, an Einstein... a Christ and a Buddha... and if the past few thousand years have seen such a stupendous growth, what shall we see in the next five thousand years? If prehistoric man, little more than an animal, has grown into the genius, what unfoldment is not possible?... the superman is with us.[4]

The image of the superman urges us to search for the 'higher' in ourselves and, from that perspective, to create our own laws. And this is pre-eminently possible in art; in our creative imagination we can build a bridge to the superman and fulfil the essential 'destiny' of man.

Man is a rope stretched between the animal and the Superman — a rope over an abyss.... What is great in man is that he is a bridge and not a goal: what is lovable in man is that he is both a transition and a descent.[5]

Understood as an artist, Nietzsche remains an inspiring figure. If we view his ideas as artistic attempts to grab the ever-fleeting truth, we come closer to his intentions. Nietzsche complained several times that he would have preferred to convey his message in music, because language automatically creates a distance from reality. In the words of the poet Stefan George: 'He [Nietzsche] should have sung, not spoken, this new soul!'

---

1. *Also sprach Zarathustra - Vorrede 3* (KSA 4,14).
2. One of the rare exceptions is Bernard Shaw, who, in 1903, wrote 'Man and Superman', a 'comedy', in which he used the Nietzschean concept.
3. Alice A. Bailey, *Esoteric Psychology*, vol. 1 (New York: Lucis Press, 1936) p. 174.
4. Alice A. Bailey, *A Treatise on White Magic* (New York: Lucis Press, 1934) p. 536.
5. *Also sprach Zarathustra - Vorrede 4* (KSA 4, 16/17).

That Nietzsche felt it necessary to battle so fiercely against Christian moral prescripts is understandable, given his circumstances and time, but we had better listen to his urgent advice not to put him on a pedestal, but, rather, to 'forget' him as a teacher and to create our own views on religion and its moral values.

Although Nietzsche was convinced that all his pains and sorrows were strictly necessary for the attainment of his higher insights, one still wonders if he did not take on too much suffering by cultivating his 'solitude on great altitudes'. The 'twosomeness' he felt with Spinoza for a short time could obviously not last because, ultimately, for Spinoza harmony, unity and bliss are to be found in the *Amor Intellectualis Dei*, the 'intellectual love for and of God', while the Dionysian 'truth' of Nietzsche remains a unity of opposites, an eternal struggle and a 'semblance' with infinite perspectives where all knowledge and values have to be dismantled and replaced continually.

No, utter loneliness, only being able to give and not receive, to live in a blaze of fire with no other being on the same altitude, this was his fate; and the price he had to pay was that he had to consume himself:

> *I am Light: ah, I wish I were night! But this is my loneliness that I am girdled with light. Ah, I wish I were dark and of the night! How would I suckle the breasts of light!... But I must live in my own light, and again drink in the flames that burst out of me.*[1]

In 1889, Nietzsche collapses when he witnesses a horse being whipped by a coachman. Eleven years of insanity await him in the care of his mother and sister, about whom he had written that their relationship with him was the ultimate challenge for his *amor fati*:

> *To believe myself akin to such rabble would be blaspheming my divinity – the treatment I am receiving from my mother and sister... affects me with unspeakable horror: here an utterly hellish machine is at work, with an infallible capacity to choose the perfect moment for bloodily wounding me.*[2]

Ironically, when he was no longer capable of saying anything coherent, it was this 'rabble' who took him into their care in his final years...

And thus, painfully and slowly, the flame called 'Nietzsche' was extinguished.

---

1. *Ecce homo – Also sprach Zarathustra* (KSA 6, 346).
2. *Ecce homo – Warum ich so weise bin* (KSA 6, 268).

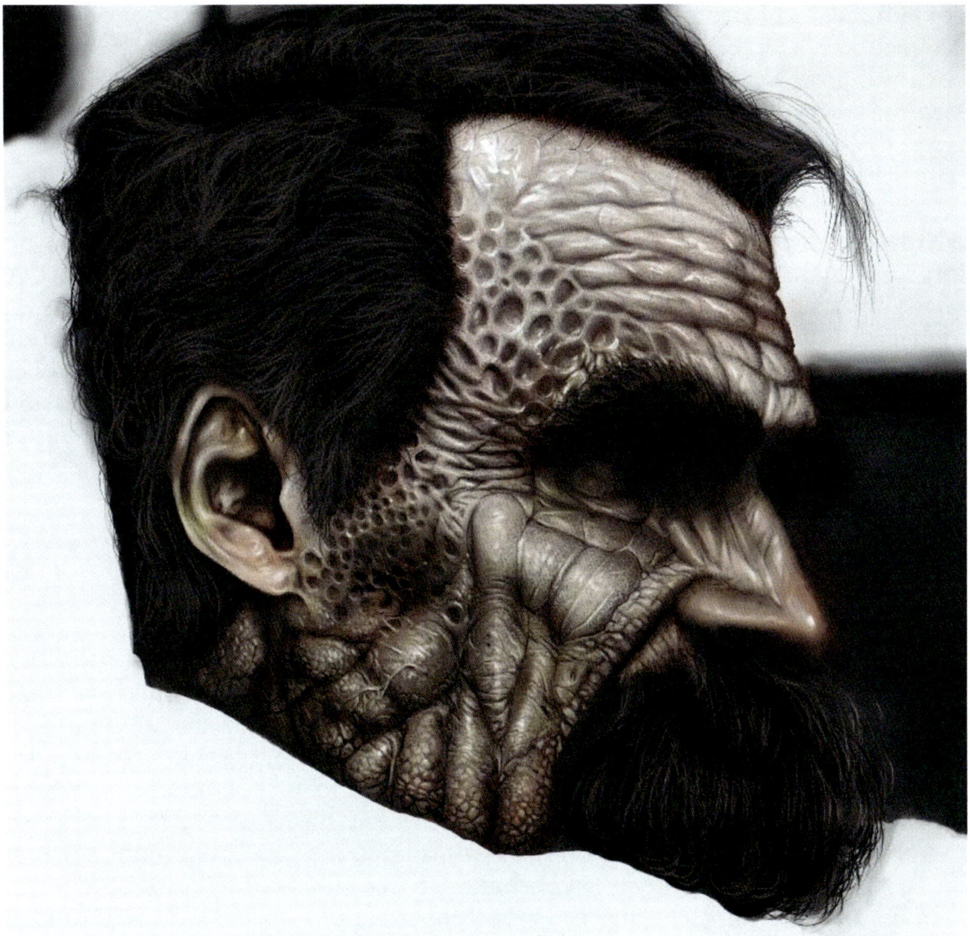

Nietzsche – Roberto Andreoli

How Artists 'understood' Nietzsche

Undeniably, Nietzsche made a great impact upon the arts of the twentieth century, particularly upon the development of expressionistic and abstract art. Immediately after his death, his ideas resonated through the words of writers and poets such as Thomas Mann, Bernard Shaw, Rainer Maria Rilke and Guillaume Apollinaire and in the works of many important visual artists and composers. The period of the turn of the nineteenth into the twentieth century was a time of upheaval in which revolutionary transformations filled the air.
Capitalism was challenged by Marx and Engels, Christianity by Nietzsche himself, Sigmund Freud discovered the subconscious and, in 1905, Einstein launched his theory of relativity.

Methods, styles and purposes in the arts were drastically reassessed. Art was no longer supposed to be an imitation, interpretation or impression of perceptible reality or an expression of the emotional self, but rather a testimony of inner and higher visions. Many artists felt attracted to this: the ground breaking example of this change, one could say, came in 1907 with Picasso's 'Les demoiselles d'Avignon' and his portrait of Gertrude Stein. This on-going revolution forced art to look inside itself and discover its own being, truth and infinite possibilities for the future: *I can envision an art that is forward-looking, that seeks its images in the future. Why isn't there such an art?*[1]

The Visual Arts

No other philosopher can claim to have had such impact on visual artists and have paved the way for the revolution in visual art in the twentieth century as Nietzsche. One could say that the visual arts underwent a Dionysian transformation, while music was becoming more and more Apollonian. Nietzsche had described traditional sculpture as 'purely Apollonian' and also as 'vanity', because it had taken the perfection of the human body as its starting point, while he characterised the art of painting as 'mainly Apollonian', because it depicted the visible reality as an enchanted dream. But suddenly, sculptors and painters were no longer trying to be faithful to natural forms and were to find their motivation in inner, passionate visions, while initially recognising only a single law: 'there are no laws an artist should be bound to'.

Also, the classical criterion of beauty was abandoned: in Nietzsche's view, an art, born out of the desire for beauty contrasting itself with ugliness is pure vanity as well, because it is motivated by human tastes and preferences, not by inner visions. Instead he wished for an *explosive development in art, unimpeded by self-expression*, while artists were supposed to be *heroic, full of erupting sexual energy and destroyers of traditional styles.*

1. Nietzsche, *Nachlaß - Sommer 1875*, 10 [13] (KSA 8, 187).

Picasso, obviously, felt attracted by these ideas. He read Nietzsche extensively and was particularly inspired by the concept of 'atavism', whereby Nietzsche claims that what is validated as 'evil' in a certain period, is often merely an echo of something once labelled as 'good' and should be considered as such again, but is currently obscured by subconscious remnants of a past morality. Examples are: religious prohibitions that have long lost any practical usefulness, unbridled sexual energy, aggression and the desire for self-expansion. Picasso himself described his 'Les demoiselles d'Avignon' as a work, in which Dionysos and sexuality play predominate roles and declared: *Nietzsche... influenced my breakthrough with this painting, which led to cubism...*

Portraits of Nietzsche were made by the expressionistic sculptors Otto Dix and Max Klinger, and by the painter Edvard Munch. However, it was Nietzsche's philosophy that inspired the founders of purely abstract art, Kazimir Malevich and Wassily Kandinsky. In his book, 'Concerning the Spiritual in Art', Kandinsky emphatically asserts his indebtedness to Nietzsche in relation to the development of his art, which he employed to *re-awaken the spiritual in man and provide an antidote to the prevailing materialism, nihilism and pessimism.*

According to Kandinsky, this new art finally became possible due to the seismic shifts in religion, science and ethics caused by Nietzsche.

Music

Although Nietzsche's own musical ideas have had no impact whatsoever – they were too traditional, fragmentary and undeveloped - it is clear that his philosophical themes have made their mark on the development of classical music throughout the whole of the twentieth century. Not all composers showing undeniable affinities with Nietzsche's ideas have explicitly spoken about this. Arnold Schönberg, for example, who indeed set a few texts of Nietzsche to music but hardly ever mentioned him in his writings, was perhaps most akin to him in the sense that, by exploring and transgressing (musical) laws, he also destroyed and recreated basic forms. Also, Schönberg's so-called 'emancipation of the dissonance', that is, no longer viewing the dissonance as a painful tension asking for resolution, but as an independent individual, might well have been inspired by Nietzsche's insight into:

> *the miraculous significance of the musical dissonance... The joy that the tragic myth evokes has the same homeland as the joyous sensation of the dissonance in music. The Dionysian, with its primordial joy experienced even in pain, is the common womb of music and tragic myth.*[1]

Later revolutionary composers like John Cage and Pierre Boulez felt also an affinity with Nietzsche, particularly with his concept of reality as a necessary process of eternal changes, in which every moment has the same importance.

---

1. *Der Geburt der Tragödie* (KSA 1, 152).

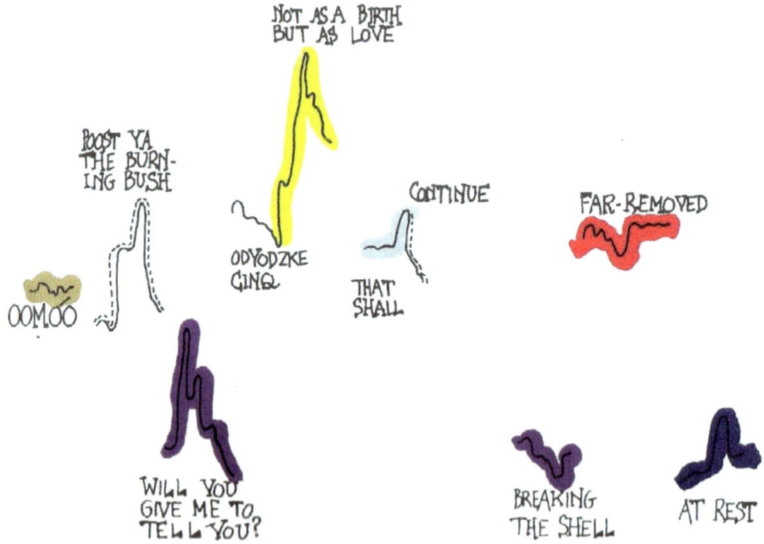

A page from 'Aria' of John Cage

But the musical genius mainly responsible for the revolution in music was, of course, Richard Wagner, whose inventions, such as the 'Leitmotiv' and the 'Never-ending melody', were an inspiration for many composers: Liszt, Strauss, Mahler, Sibelius and the young Schönberg among them. The first bars of Wagner's opera 'Tristan and Isolde', where a fluctuating tonality is applied, are generally recognised as a turning point in the history of music and a forerunner of atonality. Wagner's philosophical ideas, however, have had a limited influence, and although Nietzsche in his first writings can be seen more or less as an apostle of Wagner and Schopenhauer, it was his own revolutionary philosophy that made such an impact on many composers.

Strauss and Delius

It is generally suggested that the symphonic poem 'Also sprach Zarathustra' by Richard Strauss, subtitled 'a music-poem, free after Friedrich Nietzsche', represents a mainly emotional impression of this work; Strauss would not have had the intellectual capacity to understand its meaning. This idea is perhaps supported by Strauss' own statement that *everyone who had been hoping that I would translate Nietzsche's philosophy into notes, will feel deceived.* But translating philosophy into music is impossible, as Nietzsche himself had already dolefully concluded. However, Strauss 'understood' Nietzsche perfectly:

> *I did not intend to write philosophical music or to portray in music Nietzsche's great work; I meant to convey by means of music an idea of the development of the human race from its origin through the various phases of its development, both religious and scientific up to Nietzsche's idea of the 'Superman'. The whole symphonic poem pays homage to the genius of Nietzsche, which found its highest expression in his work 'Thus spoke Zarathustra'.*[1]

1. Strauss wrote this in response to the critics of his piece 'Also sprach Zarathustra'.

In earlier days, under the influence of Wagner, Strauss had studied Schopenhauer and admired him, but ultimately rejected Schopenhauer's idea of asceticism being the only escape route from the claws of the uncompromising primordial power, the 'Will'. Strauss started to have doubts when he realised that Schopenhauer, although seeing music as the only phenomenon through which it was possible to have a direct insight into the will itself, taught that even the musical experience could only provide a momentary escape from this raging universal force, but never a permanent one. A longer, nevertheless temporary liberation, was only attainable for the 'religious neurotic', as Nietzsche later called it, namely through the pursuit of asceticism, including sexual abstinence. Thus, for one's own salvation, one had to commit to a total renunciation of all sensual experiences, including music. Strauss opted for music and the sensual life, and rejected not only asceticism, but also Schopenhauer. In Nietzsche's writings he found what he always had been looking for: an appreciation of the physical world and sexuality, a special status for the artist as a conveyer of truth, and a rejection of pessimism. Nietzsche's idea of the eternal cycles of doubt, sorrow, playfulness and joy inspired him greatly; this became a recurrent theme in all his works, as well as the experience of being part of a wholly amoral and innocent nature. For a while he even considered calling his Alpine Symphony 'The Antichrist'.

The same criticism, namely of being an emotional reaction to rather than a deeply understood interpretation of Nietzsche's philosophical ideas, was directed at 'A Mass of Life' by Frederick Delius. However, it was Nietzsche's philosophy itself that evoked Delius' passion, so clearly expressed in this work. Delius became deeply convinced of the value of the individual and of the fundamental inequality of human beings, Nietzschean insights that had now paved the way for the superman and a spiritual evolution of mankind. Delius also saw the traditional, Christian morality as hypocritical and out-dated and shared the view that the 'higher' had to be found in this physical world itself. From this perspective he composed a ritual mass on texts from 'Thus spoke Zarathustra' as a symbol for a wholly new 'faith', namely, in an all-powerful nature, in eternal recurrence and the infinite possibilities of the future. Delius manages to express this musically in a splendid series of sunrises, impressions of midday and night scenes as a backdrop for the repeated descents of the prophet Zarathustra, seeking an audience ripe for his message.

Mahler

Mahler seems to agree with Nietzsche that music is essentially visionary. Nietzsche writes: *Has anyone observed that music liberates the spirit? Gives wings to our thoughts?… totally unforeseen, answers drop into my lap…*,[1] while Mahler expresses this same experience thus: *Strange…when I hear music I hear quite definite answers to all my questions and am wholly clear and sure… Or, really, I seem to know that they are no questions at all.*[2]

1. *Der Fall Wagner* (KSA 6, 14).

2. Mahler wrote these famous sentences in a letter to Bruno Walter in 1909.

As Mahler expressed the depth of Zarathustra's 'Midnight Song' so perfectly in his Third Symphony, one could almost say that he indeed was able to translate Nietzsche's philosophy into music. But then Mahler was a musical genius, unlike Nietzsche... Mahler named this symphony 'The Joyful Science' after Nietzsche's 'Die fröhliche Wissenschaft', and we know that reading Nietzsche (at breakfast) literally cheered Mahler up, undoubtedly due to Nietzsche's perspectives on freedom, the unlimited possibilities of the future and the essential relation between suffering and joy.

Mahler, whose psychological disposition was very similar to that of Nietzsche, exhibited the same passionate, visionary and 'religious' nature and he understood Nietzsche perfectly. From the very beginning, Mahler, like Nietzsche, was painfully aware of his grand life task, stating several times that he was *writing music for the future*. Nietzsche's severe mood swings were experienced by Mahler as well: *The highest ecstasy of the most joyous strength of life and the most burning desire for death: these two reign alternately within my heart: yes, often they alternate within the hour...*[1]

Mahler's genius succeeded in adding extra dimensions to some of Nietzsche's ideas, specifically to his concepts of eternity as 'eternal recurrence', the temporality of pain and the eternity of joy, the indifference and innocence of nature, and the loss of paradise, which, after the death of God, can only be portrayed as a child's play. We hear all these elements in many of his works: the Dionysian trance at the approach of summer, in the beginning of the Third Symphony, and Zarathustra's "O man, take heed", with glissandi on the oboe - nocturnal birdcalls, symbolic of an eternal and indifferent Nature - and a solo violin that expresses man's suffering and longing for beauty and joy. The musical illustration of eternity as eternal recurrence - in repeated, falling seconds - we find in the Third Symphony and also in his other works, including 'The Song of the Earth'. A sudden childlike outburst of exuberant joy, as in the 'bim-bam' of the boys' choir in the Third Symphony, and in 'The Heavenly Life' movement of the Fourth Symphony, where joyful naivety is coupled with a slight irony, is a recurrent theme as well.

In spite of Mahler's perhaps opportunistic conversion to Catholicism, he was, according to Bruno Walter, a *'typical non-religious man'*. Walter, however, did recognise the influence of Nietzsche: *Mahler's work and particularly his Eighth Symphony is filled with the spirit of a fiery affirmation of life.*[2]

It is suggested that Mahler, in his later years, turned his back on Nietzsche, because he himself could not live without spirituality and a metaphysical truth. This is deduced from some of the letters Mahler wrote to his wife, Alma, in which he criticises Nietzsche and urges her not to occupy herself with this 'earthenware god'. It is also assumed that the breach between Nietzsche and Wagner was another reason for Mahler's critical attitude towards the former. Although Mahler undoubtedly would have been irritated by the exceptionally violent and exaggerated ways in which Nietzsche attacked Wagner and condemned his music

1. Mahler's Letter to Josef Steiner 1879.

2. Bruno Walter, *Gustav Mahler - Ein Porträt.*

on non-musical grounds, this would not have motivated him to reject Nietzsche as a philosopher. Mahler knew how to separate the artist from the personality and did not reject Wagner either, continuing to conduct his operas, in spite of the latter's frequent anti-Semitic utterances and his outrageous, non-musical criticisms of (the Jewish) Mendelssohn. Mahler did not regard Nietzsche as a prophet of truth, but experimented with a number of his insights and intuitions. Themes such as the 'Master-slave morality' and 'masculine supremacy' Mahler considered, probably already from the beginning, as *utterly false and brazenly arrogant*, as he writes to Alma.[1] But this does not contradict Nietzsche's own advice not to turn him into a guru or accept all his ideas without evaluation; we have to create our own insights and 'morals' and adapt them continuously to the flux of life. What fascinated Mahler were Nietzsche's revolutionary and liberating answers to his own burning questions, as he formulated them in a verbal attempt to elucidate the ideas of his Second Symphony, the 'Resurrection':

> *Why did you live? Why did you suffer? Is all this only a big, terrible joke? We will have to find an answer to these questions if we continue to live — yet even if we should die!*

It seems likely that Mahler advised Alma to stop reading Nietzsche, because he feared that she was too immature and therefore would be poisoned by his ideas; just as Nietzsche himself discourages those 'that are not disposed' to read him. Mahler does seem to demonstrate here, however, that he himself was not free from an illusion of masculine superiority; in the same letter he reproaches Alma for considering the ideas she reads as her own, while, in his view, she has just thoughtlessly taken them over.

From the very nature of things, it is obviously impossible to describe which dimensions Mahler's music has added to Nietzsche's ideas. But the beauty of necessity, the innocence and fathomlessness of nature, the depth of the tension between the temporality of suffering and the eternity of joy, in short, the harmony within conflict and struggle, these, in many people's experience, are the themes that Mahler has uniquely expressed in his music.

And perhaps this then is the image that remains with us: Nietzsche, 'properly' understood or not, did indeed light a fire within the intuition of numerous artists and his influence on artistic creativity in the twentieth century is consequently inescapable. His own flame might have been extinguished all too early, but the fire that he lit and the power of his inspiration seem far from yet being exhausted.

---

1. Letter 14, 1901, from: *Gustav Mahler: Letters to his Wife*, (Berlin: Wolf Jobst Siedler Verlag, 1995), translation: Antony Beaumont.

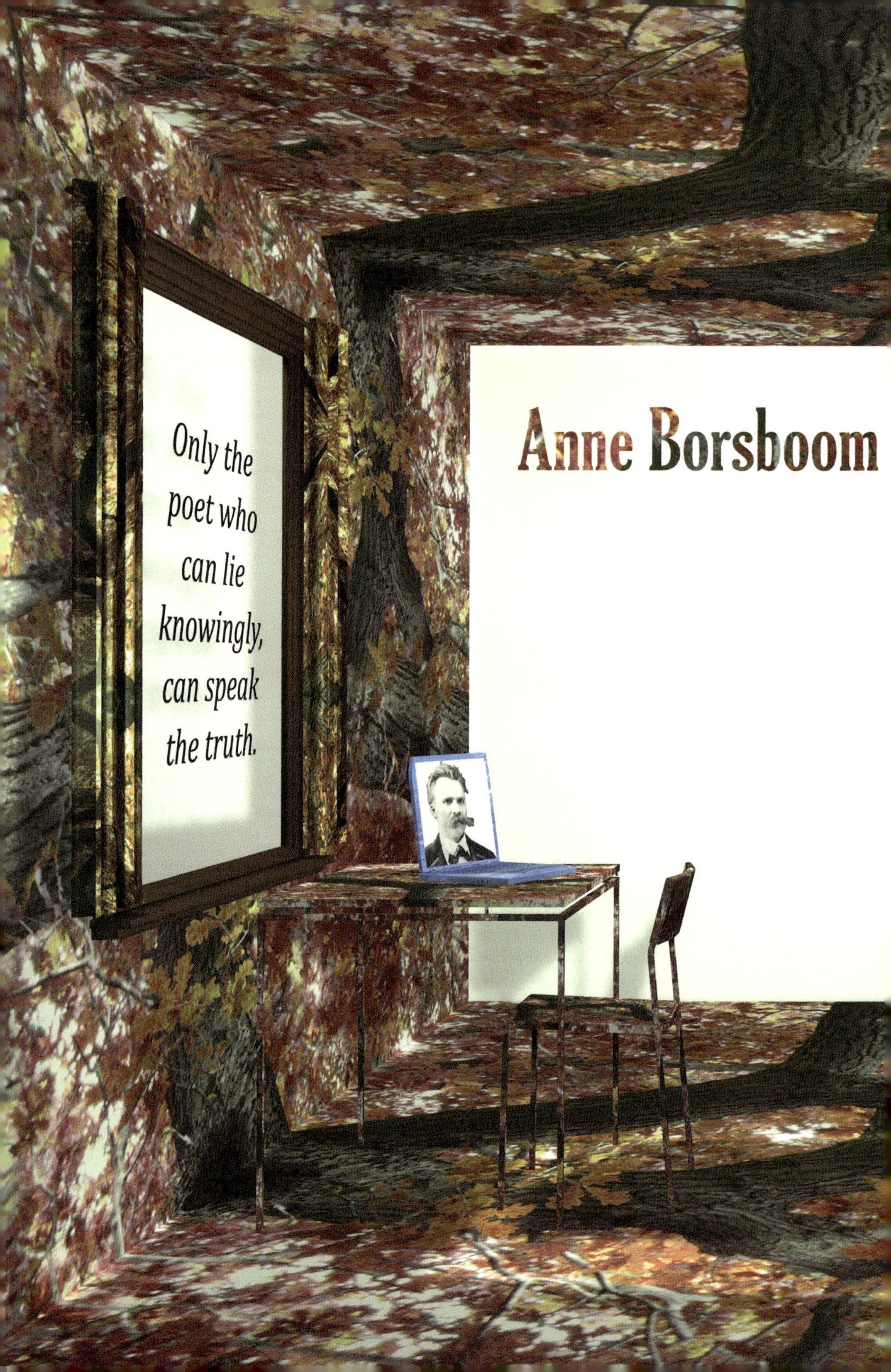
Anne Borsboom
Only the poet who can lie knowingly, can speak the truth.

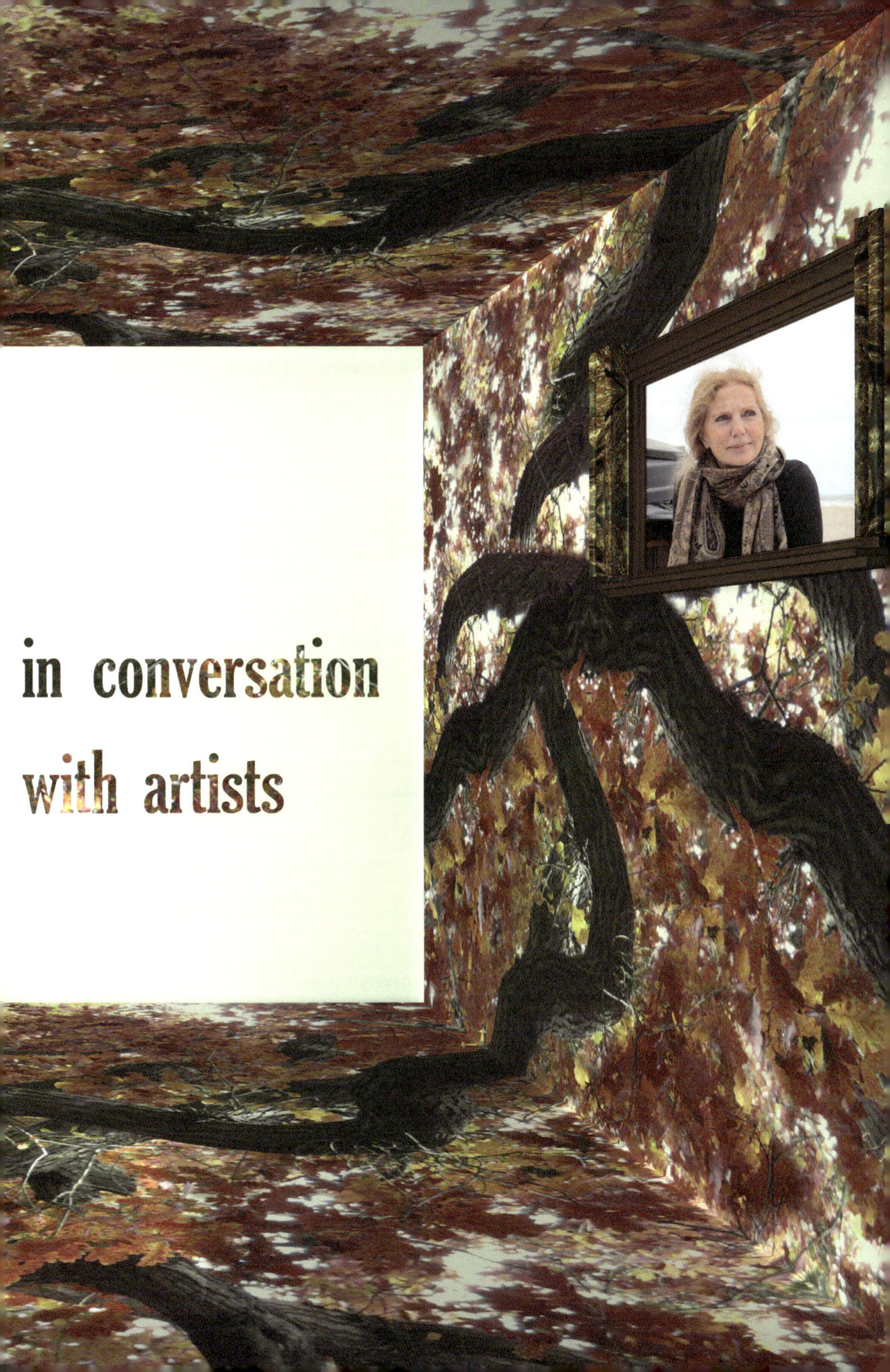
in conversation
with artists

The digital paintings of Lisette Huizenga and the eternal 'Yes'

Lisette has a large studio in a vacant telecommunications building in an industrial area of The Hague. My satnav sends me in a wrong direction and, before I know it, I've crossed over half the city. A removal van blocks the street forcing me into an even bigger detour. To cap it all, I can't find a parking space. When, much later than we agreed, Lisette lets me in, all irritation vanishes. In her bright, cheerful eyes I read a wholehearted welcome.

She shows me first some works that she painted in Florence in 2003, and we discover that we might easily have run into each other there on our way to college; while Lisette was bent over her art studies I was learning Italian. For a moment we are back in the city where one even can find art under a homeless person's mattress, and where traffic sounds echo endlessly. Here Lisette found her passion. She painted, she cried, because she thought she had no talent, started again, and one day, in a self-portrait, glimpsed who she wanted to be.

Although she has several current exhibitions, Lisette still has an impressive collection in her studio. Referring to the first painting of hers I ever saw, I comment that her work could be suitable for introducing art to children. It is as though you enter a room through a *trompe-l'oeil* where you can sit down on a painted chair. She agrees, and tells me about the difference between boys, who want to touch her work and start moving the chairs around, and girls, who are simply amazed. I uninhibitedly wander around, and see a workshop full of atmosphere, flooded with outside light and phone my son who's looking for just such a studio.
Across the street, another space is for rent.

'And now to Nietzsche, I'm curious what we're going to talk about. What attracts you in Nietzsche's work?'

My work is rather Apollonian, you can hardly call it passionate.
I was taught at The Hague's Royal Academy that the Dionysian is wild, creating a coarsely expressed gut feeling, with lots of emotion. My work is large, and light, one is drawn into it because of its three-dimensional aspect, but it remains light. I suggest space. Just recently I talked to someone who works with psychiatric patients who thought my work would be very suitable for his treatment room. And I understand that, because it's more fun to be in my virtual space than in a cold, white treatment area. I chose for the new media, because I didn't see how, through painting, I could add anything new. My thoughts go quicker than the paint, I wanted to go further and wondered: why not use the new media to let the 'painting' evolve. At the same time I wanted to understand evolution and

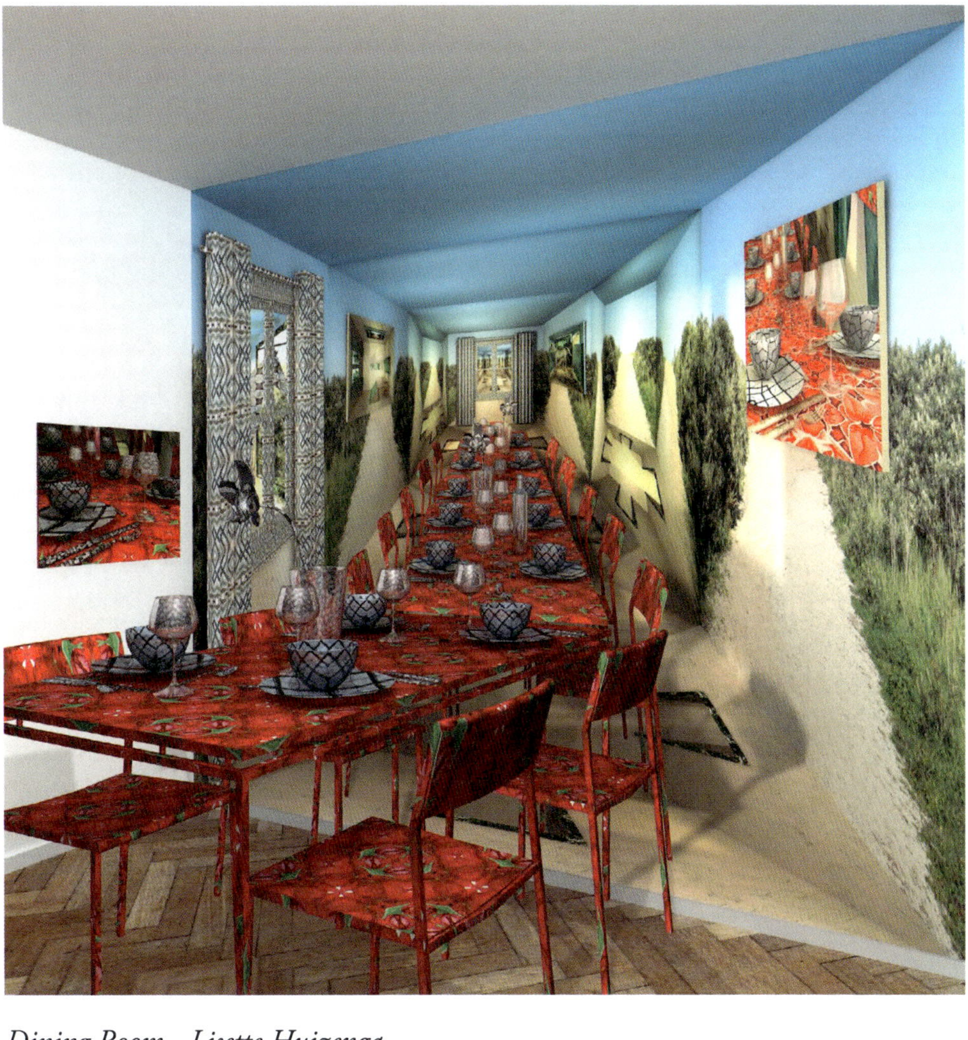

Dining Room - Lisette Huizenga

found that consciously experiencing everything in the here and now gives the most beautiful results. Philosophy, therefore, has become very important to me, I became one with it and it gave me the feeling of being right in the present. I looked for the frontier in painting, and there it was.

I was very rebellious - she says beaming - I left the well-trodden path to go my own way. Ultimately, my parents had no influence on me and became desperate when, at eighteen, I moved in with my then boyfriend, five days after we met.

> We leave her youth behind and I ask her if she already had an active interest in philosophy before this project.

I was never much of a reader, but in Florence I had a teacher who, just because of her extraordinary way of telling a story even about the simplest things that happened to her, succeeded in stimulating me. She had an enormous library and, after the first semester, when I was about to take a short vacation in Holland, I asked her what books I should definitely read. She gave me five titles, but advised me to begin with *A Brief History of Everything* by Ken Wilber, an American philosopher and writer who is seriously into 'the now'. He explains how evolution manifests itself. I was immediately fascinated with the book and, though it was difficult, I kept on reading it, over and over. When I feel a little low, I pick it up again; it's helped me clarify and structure my thoughts.

Ken Wilber developed a kind of thought framework into which he brings the whole world of existence into four domains of consciousness. He began with looking for the link between the levels of consciousness that he found in the histories of science, philosophy, politics and psychology. He called them 'holarchies'. He wanted to place sages, scientists and religious leaders under a single umbrella while doing justice to them all. To him, they all expressed truths but also contradicted each other, until he discovered that by classifying them into four holarchies the picture became coherent. It was a wonderful discovery. Wilber says that if all these domains of consciousness progressed equally, a real good world would emerge in which we could live happily. Unfortunately, with many peoples and societies some of these domains are overdeveloped and others not at all. This can lead to stagnation. For instance, look at the big corporations that pollute the environment because profit is their chief interest. These companies have evolved on the outer, material side leaving their inner realm of values underdeveloped.

> I let Lisette catch her breath and think it is not so simple. We 'Europeans' have to deal with Brussels, and don't believe for a moment that you can do as you please when you start a business, or if you have an existing company that might damage the environment. I know, from experience, they check these things thoroughly. While at the same time in the animal industry, Brussels appears undisturbed by ever more storeys being piled on top of each other. I wonder why politicians choose for more animal waste, thus higher CO2 levels. Whose interests are involved here? Lisette sighs and continues to plead her case:

Wilber doesn't quote Nietzsche in his book, but it's clear that Nietzsche was also searching for a balance between the different truths or 'holarchies'. Nietzsche lived at a time when science and industrialisation were developing rapidly. It therefore makes sense that he was looking for a balance between the Apollonian and the Dionysian, as he called it. In his time, the Apollonian, the external and rational, was being greatly overemphasised.

> I look out of the window and see ladders and cranes high above the yet-to-be-built houses and wish they would remain there because they make so impressive a skyline.
>
> 'You define architecture as an expression of the outer, collective side. What do you think of today's architecture?'

I love the evolution of structures, experiments that are well founded and well built. I see life itself as an experiment. A building must satisfy the social and cultural wishes of the time. I find the buildings of Rem Koolhaas, for instance, really exciting.

On the other hand, I dislike it when architects start imitating nineteenth-century style houses. It's so against nature. Look at the technical possibilities and the wonderful materials now available to us. We must preserve beautiful, old buildings, naturally, but imitating them is so mawkish. You don't want to block evolution, do you?

> My opinion is of no importance here, but I say that I can't help wishing architects would use more glass in their buildings; probably my longing for light after such a long winter. I don't have double-glazing, so I put bubble wrap over all my windows, and now, with hardly any light coming in, winter lasts longer inside than outside. I'm going to get rid of it tomorrow morning.
>
> I snap out of my daydream and ask Lisette what connection, as an artist, she feels with Nietzsche's theories of art, and his conviction that true philosophy and art are intertwined. I keep an eye on my watch. Two hours have passed and I know she has another appointment. She doesn't seem anxious though, but I don't want to inconvenience her.

I think that Nietzsche was way ahead of his time. Ken Wilber's book contains a few descriptions of the inner individual side, the realm of subjective thinking. It's a fact that Nietzsche doesn't pass any final judgements and that what he says is no absolute truth. He expresses a continual flow of new insights, and though many thinkers towards the end of their lives claim this is how it is and how it should be, Nietzsche has never done that, and I find that tremendously positive about him. But you mean, what significance might he still have today? I do think that he was the instigator of a huge process of recognition. This takes place not only in and through him but through the whole world and in us also. What he said one-hundred-and-twenty years ago is still amazingly valid.

Relaxing, we exchange thoughts of being happy to participate in this project and talk about the book in which the interviews will be published, both trusting that with this and her virtual art Lisette might be able to bring some meaning for the next generation.

She wonders whether she therefore should have children herself, to which my answer is 'no, your work will still be there for everyone's children and their children'... I decide to round off the conversation but still want to know what Lisette is going to create for the project.

I would love it when more people looked at art, so I'm going to make a three-dimensional dance hall set in natural surroundings. I will show a virtual dancer, an avatar of a real dancer, moving through a *trompe l'oeil*.

'I don't know how to visualize that; can you explain it a little more? Why a virtual dancer?'

This might be the beginning of a whole new form of theatre. I digitise a dancer; one could even digitise a whole performance. The dancers only need to make a single, 'perfect' performance that can then be shown in theatres using augmented reality. Thus the dancers would be free to concentrate on new experiments and new work instead of having to perform the same dance every night. How exciting the dance of the future might be in this way?

Anyway, life means taking your opportunities. I'm going to make the most of any chances. After this project I'm off to Brussels and Istanbul, and then New York.

Is Lisette's art there for eternity, will our exchange of thoughts spark off any new energies?

As with Nietzsche saying 'yes' to life, Lisette's answer is a wholehearted yes to renewal, yes to taking one's opportunities and yes to life, whatever it may bring. I think of Nietzsche and see him smiling at a woman who knows what she wants.

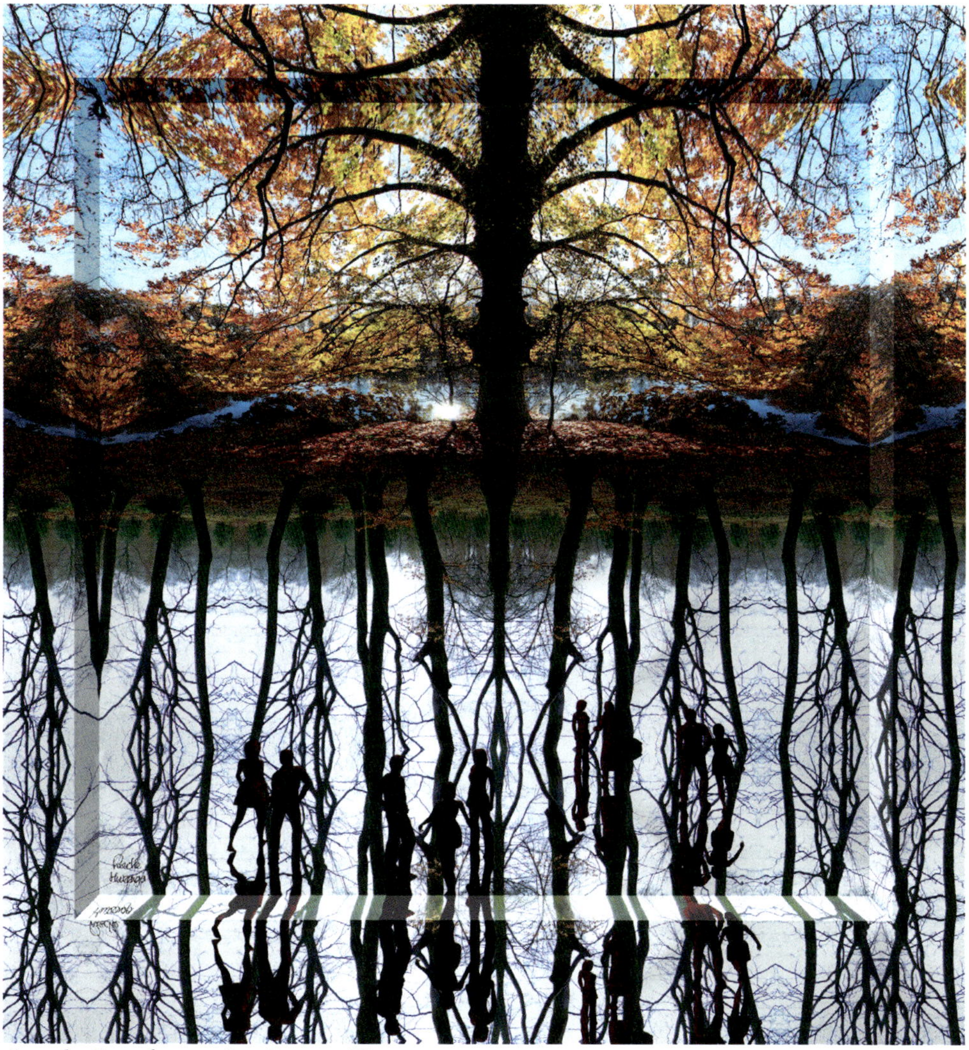

Insight Landscape 2 – Lisette Huizenga

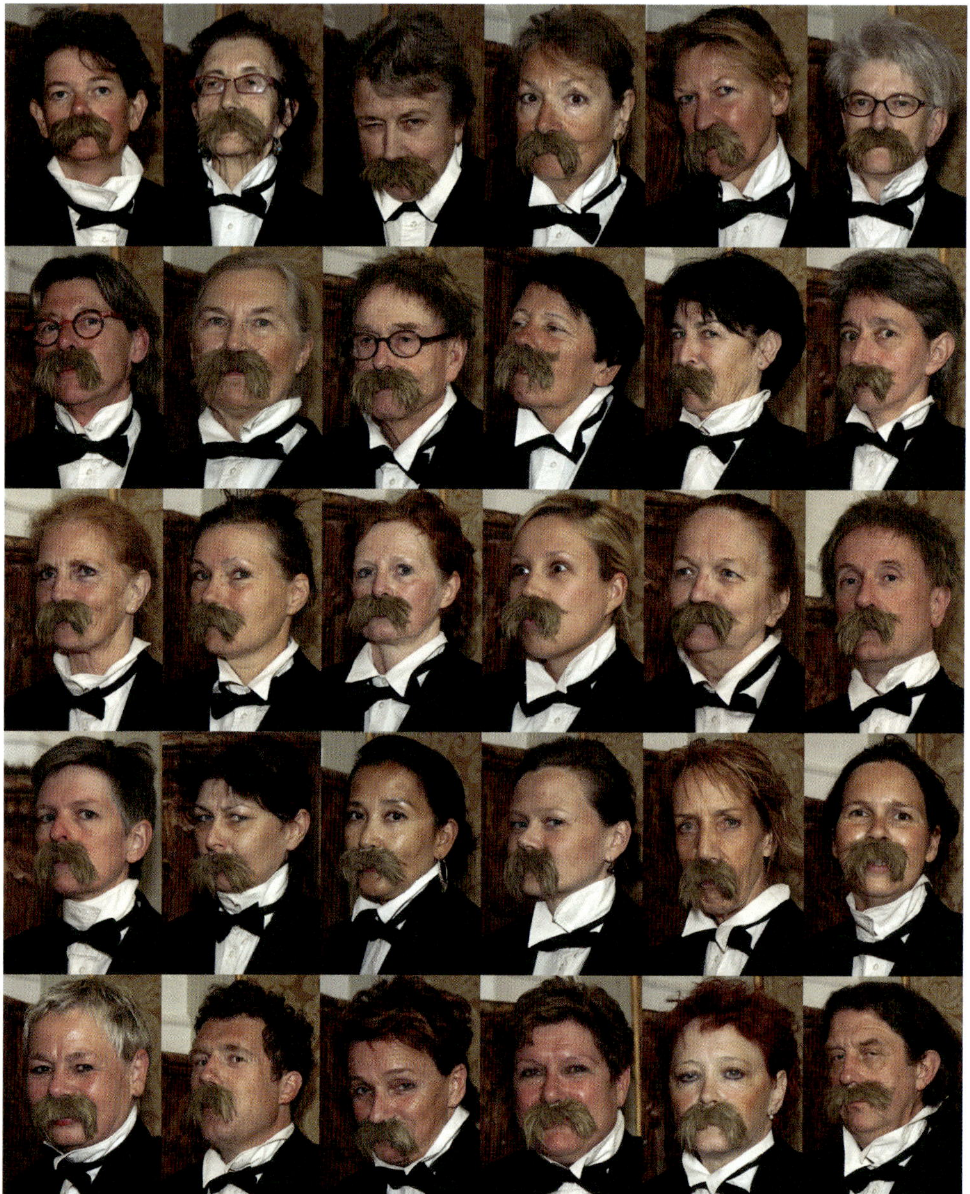

The Art of Nietzsche

'A really weird guy, this Nietzsche'

With the ease of a man who knows how to dress women, he slips a long glove onto my arm; made from old bicycle inner tubes, it's a kind of sleeve with overlapping little pieces of rubber, like the scales of a sea bass, with metal nails at the fingertips. I make a claw and growl.

Lichel van den Ende is clearly enjoying himself and takes an oval object from a clotheshorse on which two cow-heads are dangling.

These cows had a good death. Impeccable heads. Lichel elaborates on how they usually meet their end in a slaughterhouse. Torn lips, broken noses... it nauseates me. Were I to consider reverting from vegan back to carnivore, not a single doubt would remain after these horror stories.
The object is placed on my head like a hat. Attached to both sides are little wings covered with lace. 'Look in the mirror', he says. I walk across to the washbasin where a weathered mirror reveals my head. Even without makeup, dressed in an old winter sweater, I feel like a model. 'A bull's balls were in there', he says triumphantly. It's obvious where his passion lies.

Numerous pieces of rubber punched with holes were used. Recycling is important for me - he says - I never throw anything away.
I collect underpants and just got a whole bunch of them from an old friend who became incontinent. A lot of people know that I want them, so I am getting loads.

We're in a rather empty studio belonging to a friend of Lichel; she lent it him for today's interview. Above us I see a deep blue sky and below a tram crawling from a tunnel like a caterpillar, its bell jangling like an air raid alarm at a man who hoped he could just make it across.
Lichel has coffee, tea, lemonade, biscuits and cherry bonbons. I choose the lemonade, which he also serves during his shows. He no longer offers alcohol; it has too often led to chaos and misunderstandings. On the tables around us are photo albums and newspaper clippings about his projects. I spot a photo of princess Maxima and ask him when he met her.

That was during the Queen's birthday celebration a few years ago. They're really nice, they give attention to everything and are really positive, Queen Beatrix also. We had a good spot but were suddenly ordered to move way back. What a hassle! We really thought about leaving, but were finally rewarded when they came especially to see us. I had made a tree from cream puffs. I'm sure the Queen had never eaten one from Lidl before. Anyway, she thought they were delicious.

'Characteristics of the Dionysian energy are chaos, rapture, trance, intoxication… When you start collecting underwear to subsequently shred it, chaos might result. But then what? You know you can create something beautiful from the chaos. In contrast, we have the Apollonian:

order, rationality, language, beauty. According to Nietzsche, in ancient Greek tragedy and in Wagner's operas, these two energies stand together in perfect balance. Do you feel that kind of balance in your work?'

My work gives me a lot of pleasure. I dream, I process and, as soon as I run out of ideas, I get on my bike and eventually something always surfaces.

I think of my writer's block and wonder if I should try the same thing. 'Do you feel a connection with Nietzsche's Will to Power?' This project has after all been launched because of Nietzsche's thoughts and statements, so, in asking questions I try to discover what it's all about. 'According to Nietzsche, human consciousness, in its search for expansion of power, tries to control nature by forcing an order upon it that is not innate.'

Yes, quite a mouthful of fine words, but I haven't gone into any of that. I just had a compliment from a colleague who found my work very Nietzschean. The Will to Power, I've no affinity with it.

'Don't you experience a feeling of power when all your women leap into the water?'

Lichel has to laugh, saying - it makes me happy to realize how lovely all these people are to do that for me. They'll do anything to show my work! But I'd rather creep under a stone. I've never made a thing for myself; only once, when a model didn't show up, I had to hang a cape over my own shoulders. It had to be done, I reasoned. But luckily this hardly ever happens. Friends of mine once threw a horror-party for which I'd made a coffin. I lined it with satin and put it around myself; it had no bottom.
We were convulsed with laughter with the thought of a corpse knocking on the front door draped in a coffin.
Anyway, my star sign is Pisces; everything is possible, nothing must be. Chaos is natural and will somehow lead to something beautiful.

I intend to find out what 'Pisces' is all about, and go no further with that one. I think of the *Ninety-Nine Brides in the Sea* I found on YouTube.
'Didn't you find it a dreadful shame, all those beautiful wedding dresses soaking wet?'

That wasn't my project. I placed an ad in the newspaper calling for brides to jump into the 'Hofvijver'.[1] It got a tremendous response. Unfortunately, it couldn't be realised because of underwater security sensors.

I think - he says very softly - that they kind of pinched the idea from me. It's weird, but sometimes it's though there's a creative thought hanging in the air and there's nothing you can do about it - Suddenly he says in the same soft voice - I was ripped off! I bought fifty-two new wedding gowns. They were all fitted and

1. The 'Hofvijver' is the famous large lake in front of the The Hague's government buildings.

ready, then it turned out it couldn't be allowed.

It doesn't bother me at all that dresses get wet. I once splashed two hundred white dresses with black paint. How about that? I got them from a cloth company and they were really super dresses. I thought it wiser not to relate my plans to he person who gave them to me, she probably wouldn't have been too pleased.

> 'I presume you must have huge expenses for the fabrics, wages and renting of its locations. Do you have any sponsorship? I noticed in one of your YouTube videos some rattling sewing machines with brand name very conspicuously displayed. That manufacturer must have been delighted with the advertising.'

I get every possible kind of beautiful fabrics from a Belgian manufacturer who is unable to sell them. For a bridal train of a dress that had to be 2.5 kilometres long[1], I naturally needed a great deal of fabric. I called the company to ask if they could help me. They were really enthusiastic and donated all the needed fabric on the condition that I would come to them for all my future projects. You see, it costs them a fantastic amount of money to destroy discarded fabrics. Look! - Lichel lifts a heavy taffeta from the table so as to show it the right way up. He intends using it inside out because he loves black - It's really incredible how many gorgeous fabrics I've already got from them. They stuff it into every corner of my car. They're such a lovely couple, always happy to see me, incredibly sweet people. Very special! And yes, since I get no subsidies, it would not be possible to work on this scale without these donations.

The creations are sometimes extremely heavy, but they have to be worn all the same. Everyone does it for nothing. Supposing I had to pay all those lovely people, it would be simply impossible.

Suzanne (Lichel refers to Suzanne Bo) is like a pillar supporting my work. If the ceiling were to cave in, she'd push it all back.

> He shows me a photo of Suzanne modelling one of his creations, accompanied by her dogs.

During the show, there seemed to be an evil eye upon us. There were some over-zealous volunteers who kept saying: do it this way, no, not like that, like that! - Lichel lowers his voice a couple of octaves to imitate these masculine women - They started to control me. Suzanne had bought about fifty pairs of scissors, safety pins, glass carafes… nowhere to be found. I'd received a beautiful fabric from Belgium, like a kind of damask that I had used to wrap the sandwiches in and all the other lovely snacks for the picnic on the wedding train, and, at a certain moment, I couldn't even find those. I really went crazy. Everything had disappeared. However, the next day we began finding it all, stowed away behind doors and curtains after a frenzied clean-up.

---

1. Lichel's train, measuring 2,488.65 meters, is entered in the Guinness Book of Records.

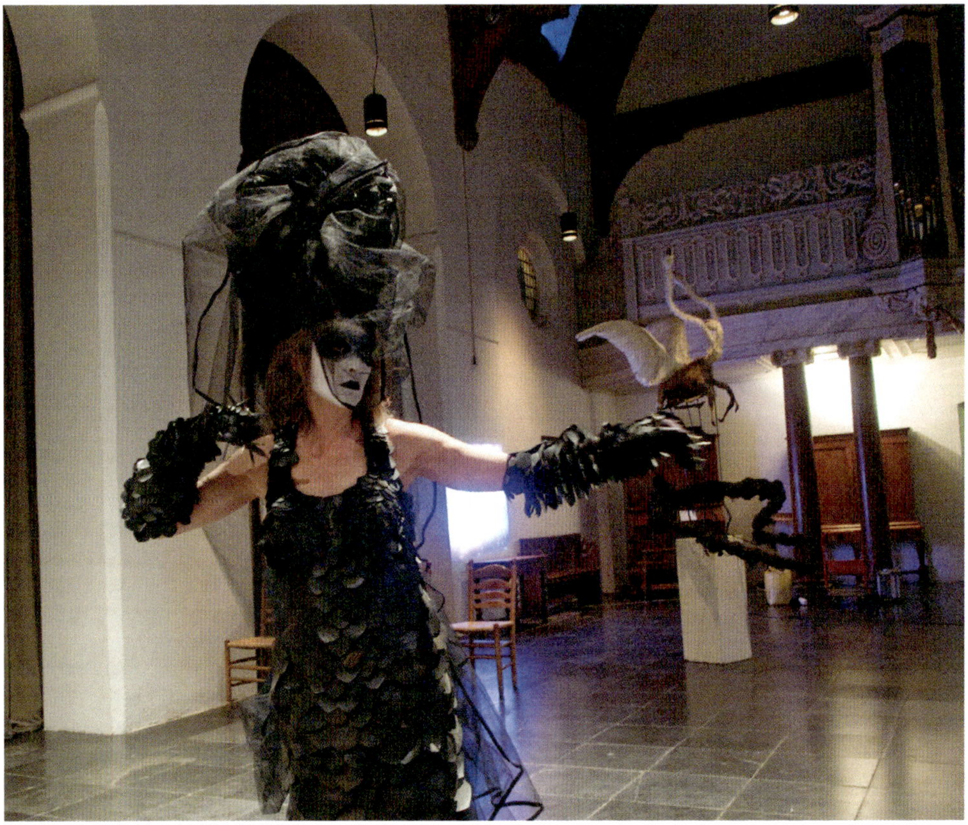

Photo: Jan van Zelderen

For a moment he seems overcome by the panic of that day, but then says - and yet, looking back at the photographs, I remember how terrific it all was. At some point I stood on the balcony of an apartment building looking down on all those white brides walking in the street. It quite took my breath away.

'Have you taken your wearable art outside of Holland yet?'

I've been to Belgium and Germany and have been invited to go to New York. But that will be such a hassle, that I'm going to pass on that one. I did go to the Wearable Art Festival in New Zealand though, in 2001. I won first prize! That was real fun. It so happened that the organiser was Dutch and had invited me to come. He thought it was about time that somebody from Holland should take part in the competition.

The phone rings and he walks away. Meanwhile I check that my sound recording is all right. Lichel puts down the phone and we browse through a huge number of newspaper clippings and magazine articles. I am impressed with the sheer volume of work he has done since 1988. When I hear a particular date, an association often springs to mind. 1988 was the year I moved to The Hague. Here, in this location, with the sky close by, the movement of life below and the sounds of a well-oiled system, here I could live. I ask Lichel if the space is for rent. He will check it out.

'What are you making for the Nietzsche project?'

A while ago, there was a fire in the neighbourhood. I went to take a look and was struck by what still remained after the fire. Shrivelled chandeliers, charred remnants of furniture. Sheer beauty. I will contact the Fire Department because I want to work with burnt chairs and other remnants of a blaze.

'Is there a reason for using this theme? Was Nietzsche fascinated with the remnants of a fire?'

Oh, sure - he sits up - I know Nietzsche found European culture nihilistic and decadent and wanted to rekindle it with new life. Anyway, he called himself 'flame'. I'm going to do the same.
I also have in mind a tableau vivant with nine dancers on a pedestal. Do you think it would fit into the entrance hall?

'If I were in charge, you could exhibit anything that came into your head.'

While I'm preparing to go, he stuffs two handfuls of cherry-bonbons into my handbag. 'I bought them for you', he says, 'just take them for the road.'

Man and Animal

I have arranged to meet **Suzanne Bo** at Pulchri Studio. Unaware of winter's return, I dismount from my bike, chilled to the bone and, with great effort, turn the key in its lock. That's what happens when you leave your gloves at home, Anne, will you ever learn? People living on their own invariably begin to talk to themselves. I continue grumbling until the door to Pulchri opens without assistance, when an agreeable feeling suddenly comes over me. Not only is Pia Simonis the face of this wonderful Art society, she is also my friend. I'm lucky she's here! She takes my purple hands in her own and rubs them till they tingle.

It's four o'clock and there's nobody at the reading table, yet, in case the place is suddenly invaded, I reserve a place for Suzanne. On top of the sculpture in the garden, a pigeon snuggles down deep into its feathers; underneath the bushes a dunnock hops around. A glass of hot water is placed before me, and I choose a black tea from a silver-coloured box. After my bike ride through the cold, easterly wind, I'm aware of a comforting warmth and remember how my mother used to rub my hands.

Suzanne enters with her two little dogs, a Chihuahua and a Maltese terrier. Knowing nothing about dogs, age, breed and expected lifespan are explained to me. They settle down like royalty onto the pillow Suzanne has brought along. An extended conversation follows with the waitress, who also has a Chihuahua and, in no time at all, several interested people are gathered around the table. The dogs, used to it all, get bored because they really want to sleep; I expect them, at any moment, to suppress a yawn behind a manicured paw. Suzanne also asks for tea.

'I looked at the diversity of art works on your website. Your works are born from the intuition, as you say, reflecting the imperfection and vulnerability of body and spirit. In human encounters, outer appearances often seem at odds with the unseen inner life. For you, this results in distorted, strange images, a discrepancy that drives you to create drawings, paintings, objects and installations. Pretty pictures don't work for you, there must always be another layer of reality. This seems to relate somewhat to the *untrodden path* Nietzsche speaks about. Perhaps this is a redundant question, but do you always do your own thing or do other artists' opinions sometimes inhibit you?'

I do just as I please and am absolutely unfazed with what anybody else might think, - she hesitates, perhaps unaccustomed with being interviewed, then goes on - used objects in particular inspire me, things already handled by people. With a new book - she picks up a small diary - I look forward to enjoying its first dog-ear. At the moment, I feel mostly attracted to the tragic, the chaotic, the unpredictable, let's say, the Dionysian.

Suddenly, she shows me a photo of a small, papier-mâché, human body attached to a rat's skull she found in the fields once.

Now it is part human and part animal and thus something dead seemingly has been restored to life. At this moment, I have an exhibition all about skin. Skin is the barrier between an individual and the outer world; it is composed of specialised cells and packed with sensors. When using skin, artists can create a whole range of impressions. But what I want to show is a human being's interior, literally and figuratively.

In this object, I also seem to see the contrast between the Dionysian and the Apollonian. The little skull beneath the small, human body has a calmness, a deliberation that expresses an almost transparent love for its origin. What strikes me then is a gaping hole just where a sex organ could have been.

'Is there a deeper thought intended here, or can I simply allow it to be what it is not? Is it for me to determine what might have been there and, can I like it just as it is? Had you any specific intention here?'

Yes, of course. Did I make it up myself, and why? It's a completely intuitive process. I collect objects I find in the street and start working with them. In a kind of trance, something can take shape. Often the outer and inner don't agree at all. Sadness and folly emerge, and I seek for a balance between the Dionysian and Apollonian energies, in a truly Nietzschean spirit!

Through the window I see a hazel tree in bloom; a female blackbird lands on one of its branches. Is she looking for a place to rear her young?

I ask Suzanne if her works are influenced by nature.

No - she says resolutely - nature has so much beauty, that I don't want to touch it. I started with figure drawing and three-dimensional work. My career as an artist began at the Free Academy in The Hague. There, you get an opportunity to work on your own vision. This Academy is not a part of the established educational system and it aims to give you the chance to deepen your own sensitivity.

'Do you want to shock your public?'

No, I don't create to shock, it just happens. I think even the ugly can be very beautiful; and the reactions to my work are quite diverse. People respond differently to little creatures with human bodies than to objects made from cow's skin. Oh yes, maybe it's good to mention that my cow skins were exhibited just around the time of the BSE outbreak - the mad-cow disease. It was a tremendous success, not least because it attracted a huge media attention!
And certainly, I can make pretty pictures - she laughs, takes a pen and with a few strokes, explaining every step, draws a small portrait in my notebook - Look, I usually start with an eye, an arm, small, with a specific colour, a few holes in the body; that first eye can determine the direction of all the rest.

Suzanne shows me a collage of torn drawings. I think back to the uncontrollable urge I had as a child to draw on everything, the wallpaper, a new, white, plastic tablecloth. Happy with this little drawing of hers, it seems a shame now that I lost this urge.

'Now that Nietzsche has an important role in your life, I assume you'll allow yourself to be influenced by the thoughts that occupied him?'

My hand lets itself be guided. Nietzsche says: God doesn't exist; God is dead. Man has to become god. But people have died because they weren't heard. The only thing they could do was to work, work for their daily bread, so who had the chance to become something else? Man is an evolving animal; man and animal are nearly the same. Man should be like an animal who still retains its natural power.

'This would mean we should make better use of our primal feelings or instincts. Nietzsche would agree to that. What strikes you about Nietzsche?'

I think of the tale of that horse getting beaten, after which Nietzsche wrapped his arms around it, crying inconsolably; the onset of his insanity. I find it such a beautiful image that I will let it be my inspiration for this project and incorporate it into a three-dimensional work.

'Do you ever doubt yourself, for instance, now, faced with a commission like this?'

Everyone can go on doubting themselves. After my mentors at the Free Academy continued saying: big, bigger, or no, no, smaller, my self-confidence finally emerged. I thought everything should follow rules, but suddenly I was free. I was amazed, it's allowed, allowed, allowed. Everything I want is allowed. I used to think you must have paper or canvas to make a painting, but you can paint on anything, absolutely anything!

The little dogs wake up, yawning. A straight, vapour trail of a plane in a clear sky promises us a night frost.

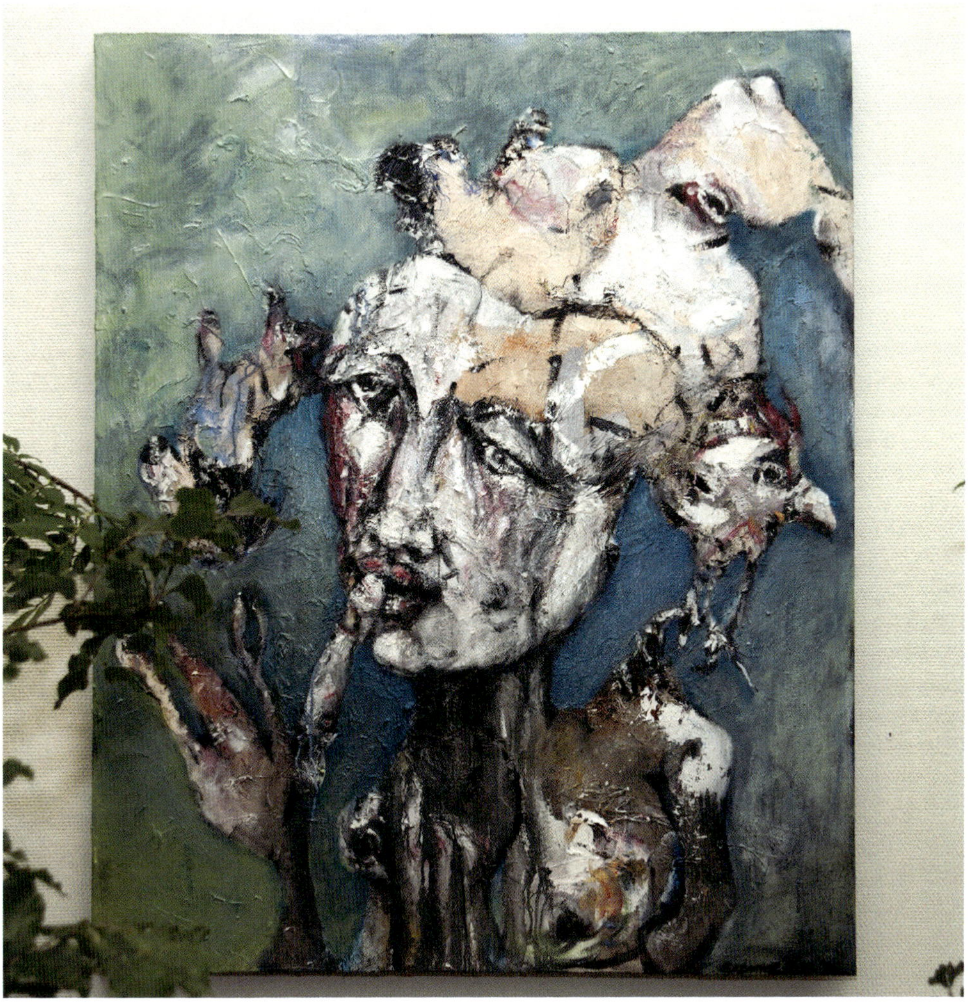

Nietzsche… nur Narr! nur Dichter! - Suzanne Bo. Photo: Arnold Cocu

Just when you think you have grasped the truth, it all slips away

We meet in the club room of Pulchri Studio, have some tea and, growing irritated by some noisy visitors, decide to walk along the Lange Voorhout to the posh Hotel des Indes where it might be quieter. The doorman accompanies us all the way along the red carpet until we become entrusted to the care of another nice gentleman in a tight-fitting suit. We continue our conversation on a soft sofa, upholstered in beige velvet. Drapes and carpet give a pleasing acoustic and we can hardly hear the other voices around us. We are impressed with this place and its domed ceiling at the centre of a huge lounge. Both of us have been here before, on separate occasions, when all the chairs were still upholstered with red velvet, the thick carpet well worn and the gold leaf hidden under an old patina. The Emperor got new clothes, just by pressing an aerosol button. But we know we want to stay here.

Ditty Ketting lives and works in Rotterdam and feels blessed to have her studio right next to her home. When we made the appointment for the interview, she had said, slightly aloof: 'I should warn you that I'm not much of a talker, I prefer to paint' and I had promised not to disturb her with any personal issues. As an interviewer, I should ask short, relevant questions but, within thc framework of *The Art of Nietzsche,* I was asked to weave my own stories into the conversations, and there's nothing I like more. I ask Ditty to tell me about her work. On her website I'd seen an impressive list of her exhibitions, Paris, London, New York, her work has certainly travelled further than between Rotterdam and The Hague.

'Where and when were you educated in the visual arts?'

From 1975 to 1980, I studied at the Art Academy in Rotterdam. I was born in Rotterdam-Pernis, and I still live and work there.

'What do you wish to express in your paintings? I see lines and colour and, above all, structure.'

In my paintings, colour and space are as essential and as all important as light. I paint in acrylic, horizontal and vertical coloured strips, not any image but a grid of colours in which I use carefully chosen colour schemes. In order to obtain the purest effect of the colours, I apply the paint evenly and smoothly onto the canvas in several thin layers. The horizontal strips continue onto the sides of the canvas to create a perspective between foreground and background.
With symmetries and repetition or interruption of the size of the strips, the rhythms reinforce an interaction between the colours. Sometimes they're closely related, creating a tension because their combination is like a fermentation as

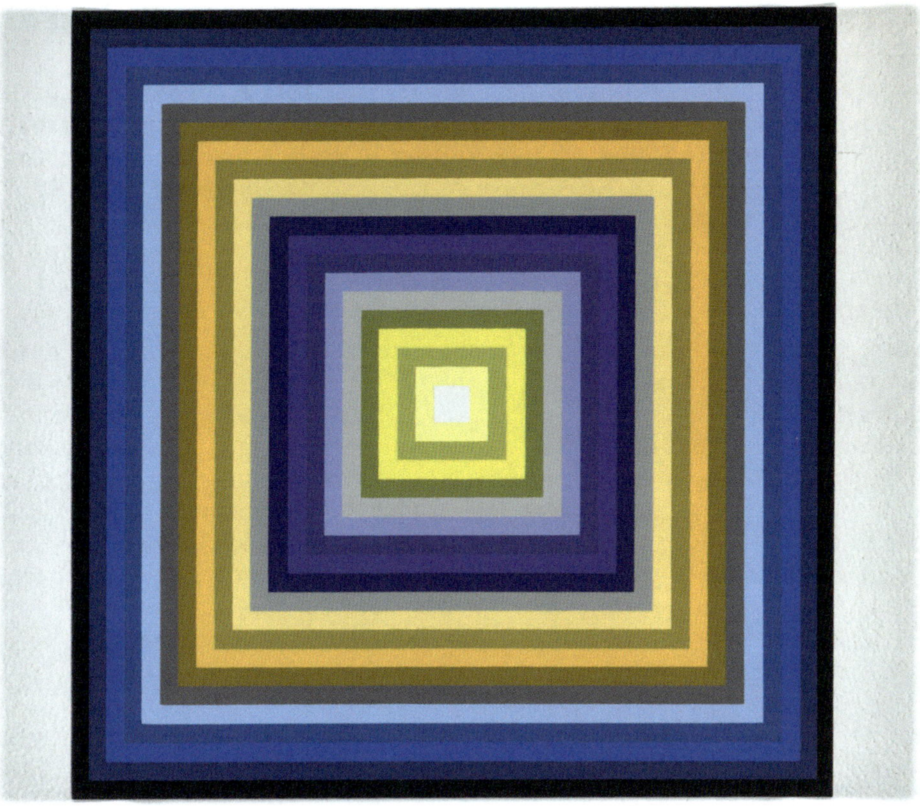

Untitled (2009) - Ditty Ketting

they move towards each other. But when the colours are complementary, they repel each other and the painting seems to vibrate. The eye darts around the canvas but can't find anything to hold onto. Also, the spectator's position greatly influences the effect of the colours; their 'truth' keeps shifting. That one could call a Nietzschean aspect of my work. At other times the colour strips make an effect like beams of light floating at different distances from the surface.

I'm impressed with the flow of her words that so clearly express her passion and specialisation. I ask her about her connection with philosophy: 'Will you make a painting or something else especially for this exhibition or present something you've already made?'

I'll show something I've already done. All my abstract paintings are based on what you might call philosophical themes, like light, truth and fluidity.
Colours are all-important to me, because they're relational. When they connect to each other in an illusionary space, they come to life. It is a recurring process, and I think I still can take it much further. I don't intend moving far from what I'm doing right now. After thirty years taking small, orderly steps within a limited pattern of colour-structures, I'm content to be where I am.

'Which artists have influenced you?'

I've been particularly inspired by Josef Albers and his non-form, the vertical bands or stripes. He was a German mathematician and artist who worked at the Bauhaus Institute under Walter Gropius. When I went to the Academy in 1975, this early avant-garde movement had become very popular once more. Artists tended towards constructivism, using geometric forms and systematic methods. In my first year, I was introduced to the colour theory of Albers. In my studio I have a book of his that is very dear to me, Interaction of Color, from 1963, and I still enjoy reading it. Next to Mondrian, Albers became my source of inspiration.

I just read a description of you as 'a disciplined, but lonely seeker'. Do you recognise that?

The work in one's studio is a lonely affair, because you can only rely on yourself to develop your art and, from time to time, to re-direct it. On the other hand, I feel far from lonely, knowing that there are many artists to whom I feel closely connected. I follow a number of them faithfully and am encouraged and inspired when talking with them in the studio and meeting them in the gallery.

The teapots are empty. I try to attract the attention of the waiter who served us. He's busy setting a table and doesn't notice me, not even when he looks directly at us. There are moments when I would love to whistle through my fingers, really loudly.

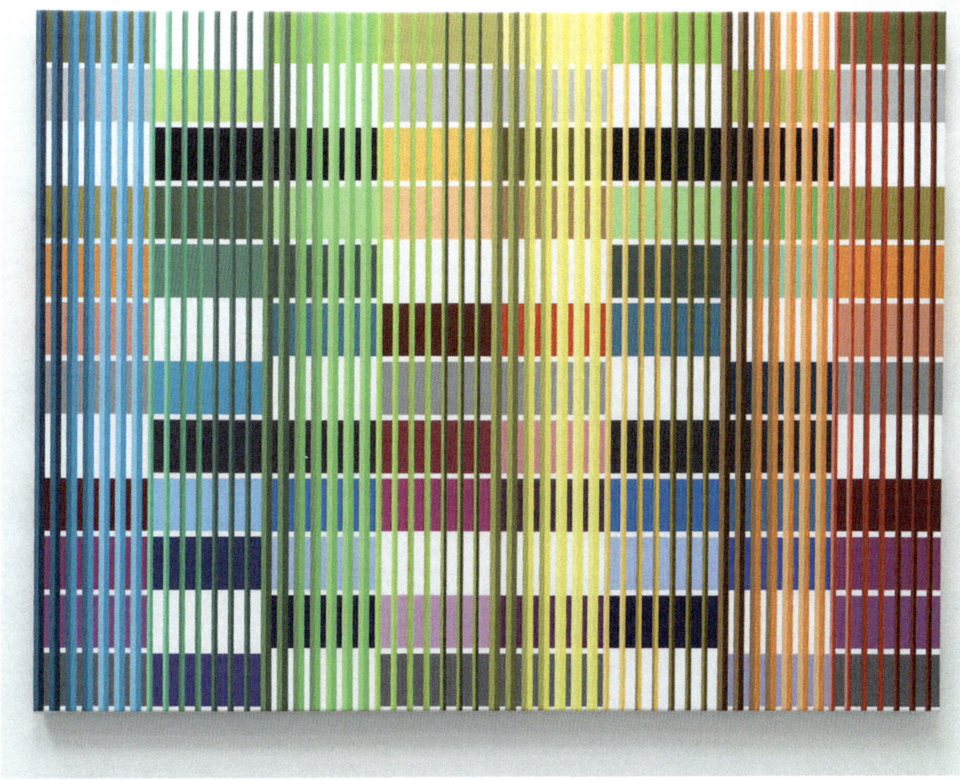

Untitled (2010) - Ditty Ketting

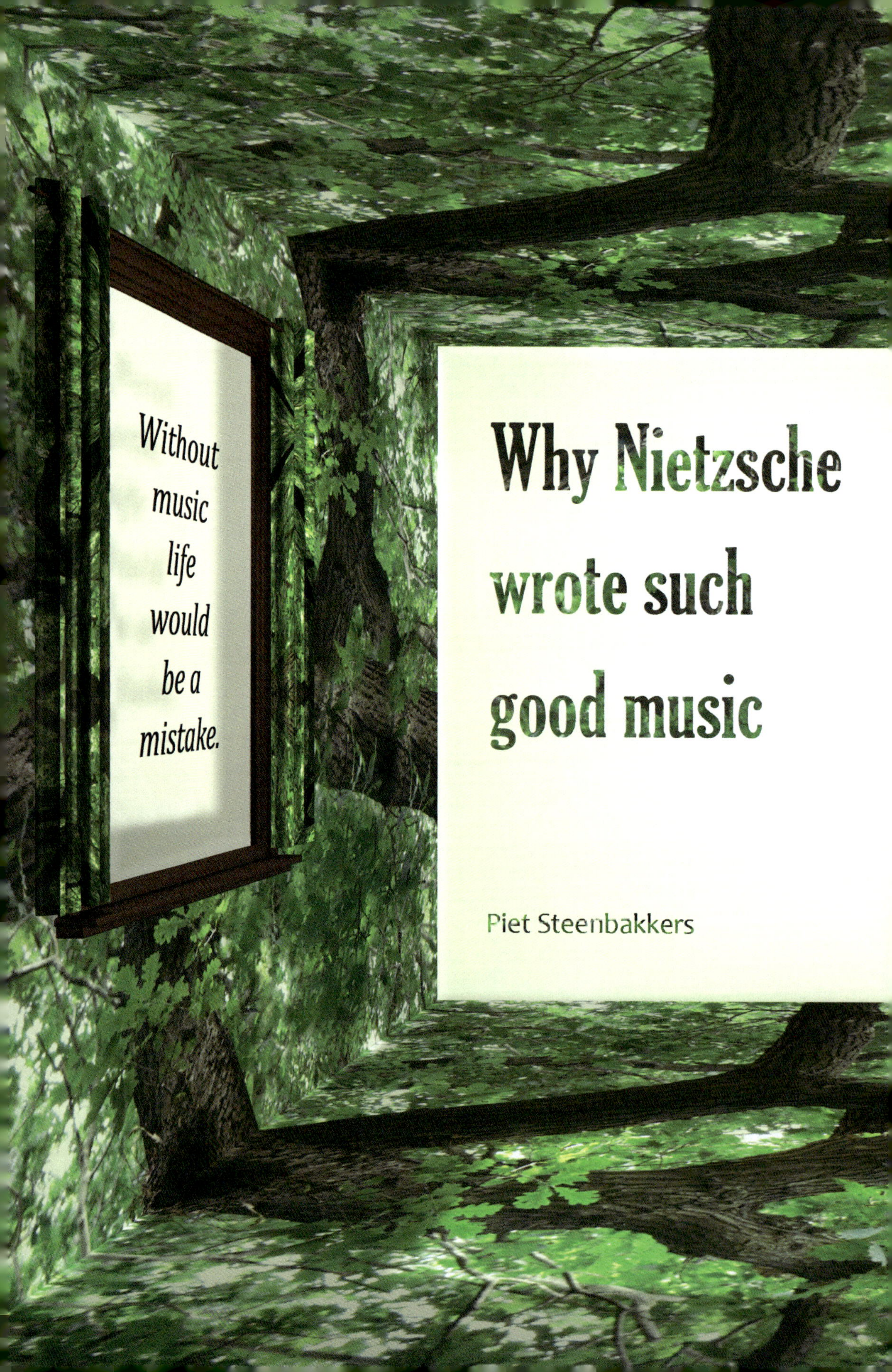
Without music life would be a mistake.
Why Nietzsche wrote such good music
Piet Steenbakkers

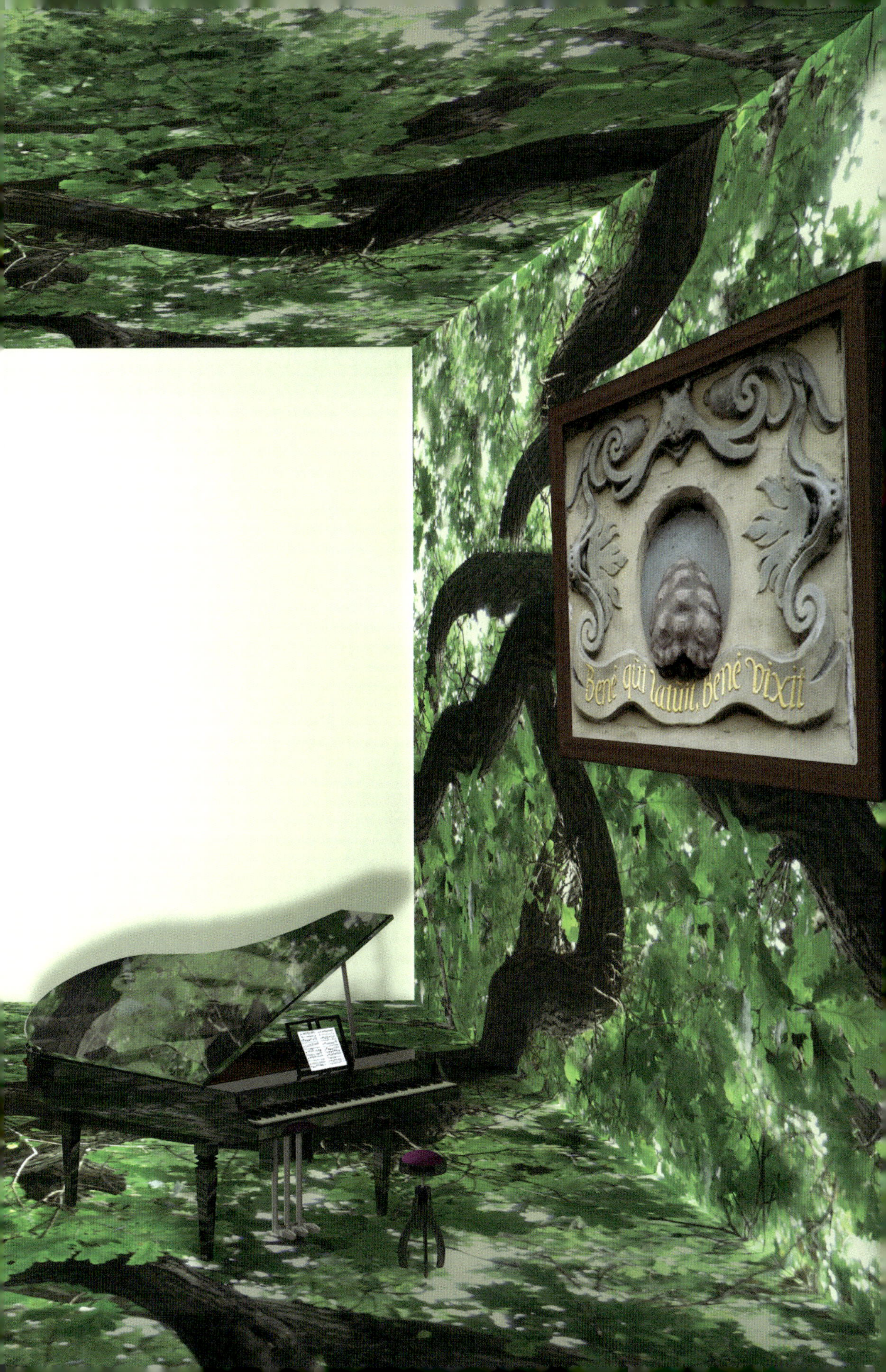
Bene qui latuit, bene vixit

Why Nietzsche Wrote Such Good Music

A title like this, 'Why Nietzsche wrote such good music', is bound to stir up amazement: did the philosopher Friedrich Nietzsche compose music? And if it is so good, why is it hardly ever performed? The answer to the first question is simple: yes, Nietzsche wrote compositions, and quite a few, too. The critical edition of his entire oeuvre, as published by Bärenreiter, comprises seventy-four numbers, some three hundred pages of score.[1] Nietzsche was not only a philosopher, but also a composer, and – so we may add – a poet and a writer, too. Whether his music was indeed so good is another matter. The answer here cannot be straightforward, and that may well be the reason why his compositions are rarely performed; more about this later. But to someone who is not unfamiliar with Nietzsche's work, the phrase, 'Why Nietzsche wrote such good music', will inevitably evoke associations with the outrageous chapter headings of one of his final works, *Ecce Homo: How One Becomes What One Is* (written in 1888–89 and published in 1908). They read, in succession: 'Why I Am So Wise', 'Why I Am So Clever', 'Why I Write Such Good Books' (a chapter in which he assesses his own books, from *The Birth of Tragedy*, 1872, up to *The Case of Wagner*, 1888) and 'Why I Am a Destiny'. The book may originally have been even more preposterous: the version in which *Ecce Homo* has come down to us was purged before publication by his personal assistant, the composer Heinrich Köselitz (1854–1918), who toned down passages in which Nietzsche went overboard with his self-conceit and his jeers at others.[2] In that sequence a chapter entitled 'Why I Write Such Good Music' would not have come amiss. Since Nietzsche had features that cannot automatically be attributed to every German philosopher, viz. a sense of humour, self-mockery, irony and a delicate touch, these chapter headings should perhaps be taken ironically. Yet no attentive reader will miss the veritable megalomania that haunts *Ecce Homo.* Combined with the marvellous airiness that is equally characteristic of this work, the result is pitiful and even tragic. In this work we hear the voice of someone who is losing his footing, slipping away into a delusion from which he will never return. *Ecce Homo* is his ultimate, ill-fated attempt to ward off his collapse. From January 1889 until his death on 25 August 1900, Nietzsche was beyond reach, lost in his mental derangement.[3] In 1888, on the verge of his breakdown, he engaged in feverish activity. Within a year, he wrote six books: *The Case of Wagner: A*

1. Friedrich Nietzsche, *Der musikalische Nachlass,* hrsg. im Auftrag der Schweizerischen Musikforschenden Gesellschaft von Curt Paul Janz (Basel: Bärenreiter, 1976). A new series for performers is now being published by Dohr Verlag in Cologne.
2. See Giorgio Colli and Mazzino Montinari, 'Peter Gast, Elisabeth Förster-Nietzsche und die Konstitution des Ecce-homo-Textes,' in Friedrich Nietzsche, *Sämtliche Werke: Kritische Studienausgabe*, ed. by Giorgio Colli and Mazzino Montinari (henceforth cited as KSA), 2nd ed. (München: Deutscher Taschenbuch Verlag, 1988), vol. 14, *Kommentar zu den Bänden* 1–13, 459–470.
3. Curt Paul Janz, *Friedrich Nietzsche: Biographie* (München: Deutscher Taschenbuch Verlag, 1981), Vierter Teil: 'Die Jahre des Siechtums (Januar 1889 bis zum Tod 25. August 1900).'

Musician's Problem; Nietzsche contra Wagner: Documents of a Psychologist; Twilight of the Idols: Or How to Philosophize with the Hammer; The Anti-Christ: Curse on Christianity; Ecce Homo: How One Becomes What One Is, and finally his *Dionysus-Dithyrambs*. Then he collapsed. On 6 January 1889 he wrote to the historian Jacob Burkhardt: 'Dear Professor, In the end I'd much rather be a professor in Basle than God, but I did not dare push my private egoism so far as to forgo creation.'[1] In the following decade Nietzsche hardly spoke a word, but when he did, it was about music. He also sang and played the piano, even though his skills declined.[2] More than anything else this illustrates how vitally important music was to him. 'Without music life would be a mistake,'[3] he wrote, and these words are rightly often quoted.

Throughout his life, Nietzsche composed and performed music. He is reported to have been a creditable amateur pianist, with an excellent musical memory and an accurate inner ear. He played with a lot of feeling and a talent for improvisation.[4] He never had lessons in composition; in that respect he was entirely self-taught. For a pianist, composing usually involves improvising. This is apparent in his many compositions for the piano, which are full of sudden turns, modulations, arpeggios and undeveloped themes.[5] Nietzsche also sang in choirs: in 1865 he participated as a bass in a performance of Handel's *Israel in Egypt* in Cologne.[6] Choral music continued to exert a fascination on him: he estimated the oratorio higher than opera. As a young man, Nietzsche wrote music for strings and choir (a motet in 1858, a mass in 1859, as well as some oratorio fragments), and somewhat later songs, too. In 1863–64 he wrote one single composition for violin and piano, *Eine Sylvesternacht*.[7] He also tried his hand at scoring, but his skills were insufficient for writing orchestral parts.

1. 'Lieber Herr Professor, zuletzt wäre ich sehr viel lieber Basler Professor als Gott; aber ich habe es nicht gewagt, meinen Privat-Egoismus so weit zu treiben, um seinetwegen die Schaffung der Welt zu unterlassen.' Nietzsche to Burckhardt, 6 January 1889, letter 1256. Friedrich Nietzsche, *Sämtliche Briefe: Kritische Studien-ausgabe*, ed. by Giorgio Colli und Mazzino Montinari (henceforth cited as KSB) 2nd ed. (München: Deutscher Taschenbuch Verlag, 2003), vol. 8, 577–578. Unless indicated otherwise, translations are my own.
2. David S. Thatcher, 'Nietzsche and Brahms: A Forgotten Relationship,' *Music and Letters* 54 (1973), 261–280; 280. Curt Paul Janz, 'Friedrich Nietzsches Verhältnis zur Musik seiner Zeit,' *Nietzsche-Studien* 7 (1978), 308–338; 308–309.
3. Nietzsche to Brandes, 27 March 1888, letter 1009 (KSB 8, 280): 'Ohne Musik wäre mir das Leben ein Irrthum.' Nietzsche to Köselitz, 15 January 1888, letter 976 (KSB 8, 232): 'Das Leben ohne Musik ist einfach ein Irrthum, eine Strapatze, ein Exil.'
4. C.P. Janz, 'Vorwort,' in Nietzsche, *Der musikalische Nachlass*, IX.
5. 'Improvisateur plutôt que compositeur,' according to Florence Fabre, *Nietzsche musicien: La Musique et son ombre* (Rennes: Presses universitaires de Rennes, 2006), 30.
6. Nietzsche to his sister Elisabeth, 11 June 1865, letter 469 (KSB 2, 61–63).
7. A recording of this piece is included in the music recordings, no 14.

That music played an essential part in Nietzsche's life is also apparent from the number of musicians (performers, conductors and composers) he was acquainted with: among them Richard Wagner, Hans von Bülow and the aforementioned Heinrich Köselitz.[1] The latter, whom he had met as a student in Basle, became his personal secretary. It was Nietzsche who dubbed him 'Peter Gast', the name by which he is known as a composer. Köselitz did not profit from his close ties with Nietzsche, however. He certainly had talents, but Nietzsche grossly overrated him, presenting him as the new Mozart. Because so many musicians took their cue from Nietzsche, the expectations were such that Köselitz could not meet them. This undeservedly gave him a bad name as a composer: his works have fallen into complete oblivion.[2]

Nietzsche wrote many of his compositions as contributions to 'Germania', a fellowship he had established in 1860 with two school friends, Gustav Krug and Wilhelm Pinder, and which would last for three years. Each of the three members was obliged to submit a creative product every month. Nietzsche characteristically contributed mainly musical creations.[3] It was in this fellowship, too, that Nietzsche eventually yielded to Wagner's music, after having played a piano score of *Tristan und Isolde*.

Within himself, Nietzsche experienced complex and rich music, but it was his tragedy that he did not have the skills to turn it into sound – neither as a pianist nor as a composer. 'Has it been noticed that music liberates the spirit? gives wings to thought? that one becomes more of a philosopher the more one becomes a musician?'[4] If that is right, and if Nietzsche was indeed musically gifted, the question arises *why* he did not invest in developing his talents. A question like this will presumably never be answered satisfactorily: in fact it comes down to the comprehensive question why things did go the way they went. Yet we can designate several biographical factors that may have been operative here. I will point out three of these.

For a start, Nietzsche's unmistakable musicality was not his only talent, nor his most important one. His favoured vehicle of expression had always been

1. In addition, Curt Paul Janz also mentions the musicians Hermann Levi, Arthur Nikisch, Carl Fuchs, Hugo von Senger, Friedrich Hegar, Alfred Volkland, Hans Huber, Louis Kelterborn, Hermann Götz; and he points out that Nietzsche had strong musical ties with his friends, too: thus he often played piano duets with Franz Overbeck. See Janz, 'Die Kompositionen Friedrich Nietzsches,' *Nietzsche-Studien* 1 (1972), 173–184; 175.
2. See F.R. Love, *Nietzsche's Saint Peter: Genesis and Cultivation of an Illusion* (Berlin/ New York: De Gruyter, 1981).
3. Janz, 'Die Kompositionen Friedrich Nietzsches,' 174.
4. 'Hat man bemerkt, dass die Musik den Geist *frei macht*? dem Gedanken Flügel giebt? dass man um so mehr Philosoph wird, je mehr man Musiker wird?' *Der Fall Wagner* §1 (KSA 6, 14). The English translation given here is Walter Kaufmann's; quoted from *The Nietzsche Reader*, ed. by Keith Ansell Pearson and Duncan Large (Oxford: Blackwell, 2006), 453.

language, in all its applications. 'Nietzsche's aim is to make music with language, thoughts and concepts, as best he can.'[1] His philosophical works are at the same time literary texts of exceptional quality. In them, he employs all sorts of forms: aphorisms, parables, poems, stories, sermons. I already pointed at the lightness that characterizes many of his texts. It is not without significance that he compared himself in *Ecce homo* with Heinrich Heine: 'One day it will be said that Heine and I have been the top-ranking artists of the German language – at an incalculable distance from everything that mere Germans have done with it.'[2] I will return to Nietzsche's poetry. A point to remember is that with Nietzsche all these different literary forms never stand on their own. One always senses in these diverging registers the urgency with which he searches for expressions of the titanic thoughts that struggle for priority. In the final analysis, everything he does is subordinate to his philosophical mission.[3] This zeal had seized him when he read Arthur Schopenhauer's major work, *The World as Will and Representation.* Nietzsche was then a young professor of Greek in Basle. The double influence of Schopenhauer's philosophy and Wagner's music resulted in his own first philosophical work, *The Birth of Tragedy from the Spirit of Music,* in 1872. This was Nietzsche's farewell to philology: from now on he expressed himself in a decidedly individual, passionate and visionary voice, in which historiography, philosophy and fiction coalesced. Although in the course of time the direction of his mission did undergo several changes,[4] his zeal only increased. That is also why he always restlessly pulled out all the stops. He no longer had time nor the inclination to apply himself to the discipline of a long musical training.

In addition, Nietzsche's health deteriorated and became ever more of an impediment. It forced him to resign from his chair in Basle. Life became

1. 'Nietzsche will, so gut es geht, mit Sprache, Gedanken und Begriffen musizieren.' Thus Rüdiger Safranski, *Friedrich Nietzsche: Biograpie seines Denkens* (München: Hanser, 2000), 9.
2. 'Man wird einmal sagen, dass Heine und ich bei weitem die ersten Artisten der deutschen Sprache gewesen sind – in einer unausrechenbaren Entfernung von Allem, was blosse Deutsche mit ihr gemacht haben.' *Ecce homo*, 'Warum ich so klug bin' §4 (KSA 6, 286).
3. I am therefore inclined to agree with the (admittedly speculative and hypothetical) assessment by Janz that Nietzsche, even if he had pursued a musical career, would still have become the philosopher Nietzsche (Janz, 'Friedrich Nietzsches Verhältnis zur Musik seiner Zeit,' 309–310).
4. It is not uncommon to divide Nietzsche's output into three stages that show not only a chronological but also a thematic coherence: 1872–1876, 1878–1882 and 1883–1888. The first period starts with *The Birth of Tragedy* and is concluded with *Untimely Meditations.* The dominating influences here are Schopenhauer and Wagner. The second period comprises three works: *Human, All Too Human: A Book for Free Spirits, Daybreak* and *The Gay Science.* His perspective then is especially that of the enlightened 'free spirit': critical, unmasking, scientific. In the third period, inaugurated by *Thus Spoke Zarathustra,* he takes issue with the quest for truth itself, and his tone becomes prophetic, religious and apocalyptic. Nietzsche's voice is eventually silenced by his madness.

increasingly arduous for him. Nietzsche started roaming. His eyesight became so poor and his migraines so bad that there were long intervals in which he could only read or write for a few hours a day. From then on Nietzsche had to conserve energy. That explains, at least in part, his preference for aphorisms and other fragmentary literary forms. If we take this into account, Nietzsche's productivity was miraculous. But there was no room left to develop his other talents. Thus, he seriously considered studying physics in Paris or Vienna, but had to abandon the idea.[1] Playing the piano also suffered from these increasingly severe limitations. His fighting spirit, however, was not affected – quite the contrary: 'What does not kill me, makes me stronger', as he puts it in the famous aphorism *From the War School of Life*.[2]

This brings us to the third element that thwarted Nietzsche's musical development. Already from his early interpretation of Greek culture as dominated by a spirit of *agon*, of contest, a pervasive feature of his thought is the idea that overcoming resistance is a necessary incentive in order to unleash energy. He even saw his own physical decay as a challenge. As if this misfortune did not yet suffice, Nietzsche also had a knack of rubbing people up the wrong way. This is not to suggest that he alone was to be blamed for the many quarrels he had in his life. An exemplary case is the decline of his friendship with Wagner. Initially Nietzsche adored him. That a rift came between them was due at least as much to Wagner's peremptory personality as to Nietzsche's own problematic character. But in Nietzsche's universe, alienation and even hostility were not considered to be fundamentally at odds with friendship. The aphorism *Stellar Friendship* clearly expresses this:

> *We were friends, and have become strangers to each other. But this is as it should be, and we do not want to conceal or obscure this to ourselves, as though it was something to be ashamed of. [...] There is probably some immense, invisible curve and stellar orbit in which our diverging paths and goals are perhaps comprehended as small stages of the way – let us rise to this thought! But our life is too short, and our power of vision too poor to be more than friends in that sublime possibility. And so we want to believe in our stars, even if we were to be each other's enemies on earth.*[3]

---

1. Lou Andreas-Salomé, *Nietzsche in seinen Werken* [1894], ed. by Ernst Pfeiffer (Frankfurt/M: Insel, 2000), 257.
2. 'Was mich nicht umbringt, macht mich stärker,' *Götzen-Dämmerung*, 'Sprüche und Pfeile' 8 (KSA 6, 60).
3. 'Wir waren Freunde und sind uns fremd geworden. Aber das ist recht so und wir wollen's uns nicht verhehlen und verdunkeln, als ob wir uns dessen zu schämen hätten. [...] Es giebt wahrscheinlich eine ungeheure unsichtbare Curve und Sternenbahn, in der unsere so verschiedenen Strassen und Ziele als kleine Wegstrecken einbegriffen sein mögen, – erheben wir uns zu diesem Gedanken! Aber unser Leben ist zu kurz und unsere Sehkraft zu gering, als dass wir mehr als Freunde im Sinne jener erhabenen Möglichkeit sein könnten. – Und so wollen wir an unsere Sternen glauben, selbst wenn wir einander Erden-Feinde sein müssten.' *Die fröhliche Wissenschaft*, aphorism 279 (KSA 3, 524).

Mazzino Montinari applies this aphorism explicitly to the broken friendship with Wagner: in a way, the rift has been a homage, too.[1] The inclination to pester his friends also took its toll on his music. On the one hand Nietzsche was well aware of his limitations, but on the other he was not prepared to accept anyone's advice. Thus he was insensitive to professional criticisms of his *Manfred-Meditation* for piano duet. Nietzsche explicitly proffered this piece to teach Robert Schumann a lesson: it was a 'counter overture' to *Manfred*, opus 115 ('against this dulcet Saxon').[2] Yet Nietzsche's composition had been picked to pieces by the pianist and conductor Hans von Bülow, which resulted in a permanent estrangement between the two. This did not keep Nietzsche from sending the piece to the conductor Friedrich Hegar, who rejected it as well.[3]

In this context Nietzsche's attitude towards Heinrich Köselitz, also known as Peter Gast, is telling. At his request, Gast wrote a version for choir and orchestra of Nietzsche's song *A Prayer to Life,* to lyrics by Lou Salomé.[4] Gast's adaptation was called *A Hymn to Life*. Nietzsche had it printed immediately, convinced as he was of its merits. He wanted it to be performed at his funeral. But Gast was a professional musician who tried to purge the composition from amateurish faults, only to be chided by Nietzsche.[5] It did not cost Nietzsche the friendship and support of Gast, who always remained loyal to him. But this disregard of well-intended advice and justified criticism by professional musicians does illustrate Nietzsche's antagonistic character. That did not contribute to his musical flourishing either.

So far I have only highlighted the problematic aspects of Nietzsche's relation to music. What about the credit side? If we are willing to look at Nietzsche's creativity as a philosopher, writer, poet and composer as a unity rather than as isolated activities, many things fall into the right place. At two distinct moments, Nietzsche exerted a profound influence on artists: with *The Birth of Tragedy* (1872) and with *Thus Spoke Zarathustra* (1883–85). The first work is closely connected with two very fertile sources that, shortly afterwards, Nietzsche struggled to break away from: Schopenhauer's metaphysics of the will and Wagner's musical revolution. In Schopenhauer's influence, music played an important part, too. According to Schopenhauer the world's innermost essence is a blindly raging, all devouring will that we cannot face without trembling – except in art, and particularly in the highest form of art, music. For it is only in music that the will, as the foundation of the world, can address us without terrifying us: instead, it will give us comfort and peace, because we can then liberate ourselves from the anxiety about our individual preservation – that is what music can do.[6] The combination

1. Mazzino Montinari, 'Nietzsche und Wagner vor hundert Jahren,' *Nietzsche-Studien* 7 (1978), 288–308; 301–302.
2. *Ecce homo*, 'Warum ich so klug bin,' § 4 (KSA 6, 286).
3. Fabre devotes an entire chapter to 'L'Affaire Manfred': *Nietzsche musicien*, 83–112.
4. The music recordings contain a version for soprano and piano, no 15.
5. For the whole story, see Fabre, *Nietzsche musicien*, *'De l'Hymne à l'amitié à l'Hymne à la vie,'* 113–146.
6. The theory of the will as the metaphysical foundation of the world is elaborated by Schopenhauer in Book II of *The World as Will and Representation.* His aesthetic

of a metaphysics of the will and an aesthetics that culminated in music as the ultimate form of art fascinated Nietzsche, and Wagner too, for that matter. With *The Birth of Tragedy*, Nietzsche blew up his academic career. After an attack by the brilliant young scholar Ulrich von Wilamowitz-Moellendorff, Nietzsche was no longer taken seriously as a philologist.[1] But the book immediately established his name as a philosopher, with its visionary plea for a liberating art, the restoration of the disturbed balance between the Dionysian and the Apollonian forces in culture by means of Wagnerian music. It had a particular impact on all kind of artists. There were no immediate effects in music, though. Soon after the book's publication, Nietzsche started to distance himself from his former adoration of Wagner. For a while, he had been part of the Wagner coterie, but he came to dislike the composer's theatrical affectations.[2] The conflict between them escalated when Nietzsche tried to convert Wagner to Johannes Brahms's music; eventually Wagner kicked him out of the house.[3] Their quarrel also involved a fundamental disagreement over the direction music should take: autonomous, as in the past and in Brahms, or narrative, mythological, programmatic, as in Wagner. In his thoughts about musical theory, Nietzsche developed a marked preference for melody over harmony. It will be a matter of coincidence that another composer-philosopher, Jean-Jacques Rousseau, had put the same issue at stake in his quarrel with Jean-Philippe Rameau. Nietzsche adduced his preference for melody as the reason why he turned away from Wagner and towards Bizet's *Carmen* as the pinnacle of Italianate music.[4] For Nietzsche (again as for Rousseau) the Italian musical tradition was eminently lucid and melodic.

The second moment that Nietzsche's philosophy inspired artists and composers was when he published his *Thus Spoke Zarathustra*, a work he himself dubbed a 'symphony' – in *Ecce homo* he wrote: 'Perhaps the whole of *Zarathustra* can be reckoned as music'.[5] In this same period, he was working on his *Hymnus an das Leben*. Around 1900, *Zarathustra* had a huge impact on the cultural climate in

---

theory, featuring music as the highest form of art, is expounded in Book III.

1. The major texts of this polemic have been collected in D*er Streit um Nietzsches Geburt der Tragödie: Die Schriften von Erwin Rohde, Richard Wagner, Ulrich von Wilamowitz- Möllendorff*, ed. by Karlfried Gründer (Hildesheim: Olms, 1969).
2. See, for instance, Nietzsche's remarks on Wagner's 'schauspielerische Urbegabung' in the fourth Unfashionable Observation, 'Richard Wagner in Bayreuth', § 7 (KSA 1, 466–472); more disparagingly: *Die fröhliche Wissenschaft* § 368 (KSA 3, 617): 'Wagner war umgekehrt wesentlich Theatermensch und Schauspieler, der begeistertste Mimomane, den es gegeben hat, auch noch als Musiker!'; *Der Fall Wagner,* § 8 (KSA 6, 29): 'Der Schauspieler Wagner ist ein Tyrann, sein Pathos wirft jeden Geschmack, jeden Widerstand über den Haufen.'
3. Thatcher, 'Nietzsche and Brahms,' 263–264.
4. In *The Case of Wagner*, §§ 1–2 (KSA 6, 13–16) and *Beyond Good and Evil*, §§254–255 (KSA 5, 200–201) and elsewhere, Nietzsche presents Bizet as the archetypal melodic composer, and southern music as distinguished by its clarity ('limpidezza', KSA 6, 15; 'Himmels-Helle', KSA 5, 201). See also Janz, 'Friedrich Nietzsches Verhältnis zur Musik seiner Zeit,' 323–324
5. 'Man darf vielleicht den ganzen Zarathustra unter die Musik rechnen.' KSA 6, 334.

Europe. Many artists, writers and composers identified themselves, on account of their creativity, with the *Übermensch*. I know of no other philosopher who created such a stir in music.[1] His texts have often been set to music, and there are numerous compositions that refer emphatically to Nietzsche, for example the tone poem *Also sprach Zarathustra*, Op. 30 (1896) by Richard Strauss; the Third Symphony in D minor (1902) by Gustav Mahler, with for its fourth movement ('Sehr langsam, misterioso': Very slowly, mysteriously) an orchestral setting for alto solo of Nietzsche's poem 'O Mensch! Gib acht!'; or *A Mass of Life* (1907) by Frederick Delius. Arnold Schönberg, Anton Webern, Carl Orff and Wolfgang Rihm also set to music material taken from Nietzsche. In the body of music inspired by Nietzsche, *Zarathustra* constitutes a large share. It gave rise to a number of large-scale and occasionally even pompous compositions. Though that is certainly one aspect of Nietzsche, there is clearly another side to him, too – one of lightness and dance:

Für Tänzer	*For Dancers*
Glattes Eis	Slippery ice
Ein Paradeis	Is paradise
Für den, der gut zu tanzen weiss. [2]	For those whose dancing skills suffice.

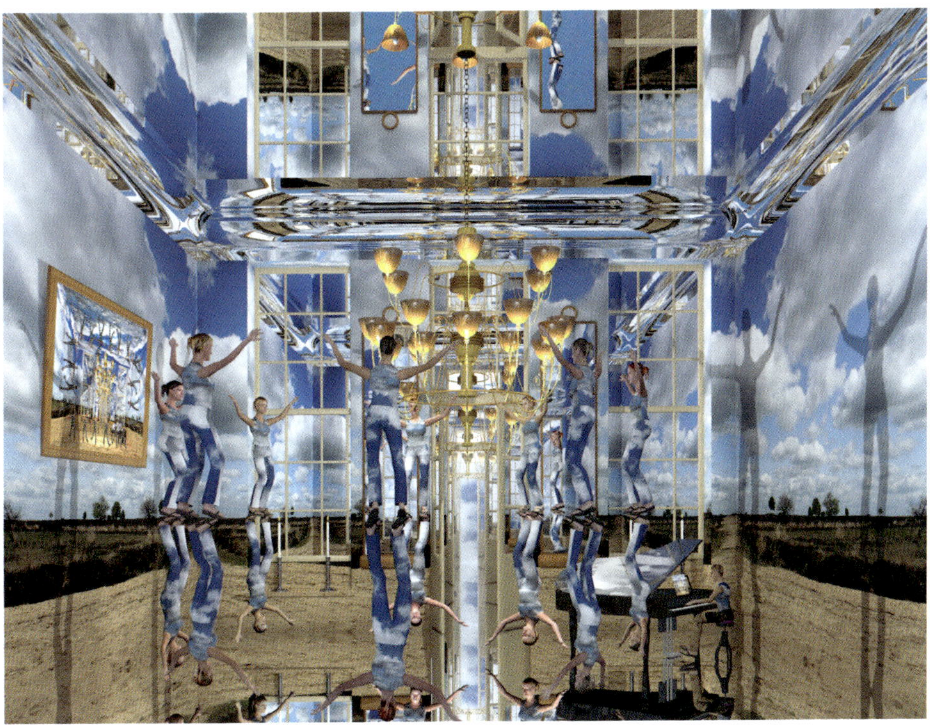

Thinking Dancing – Lisette Huizenga

1. David S. Thatcher provides an inventory of all compositions influenced by Nietzsche in an article in three instalments: 'Musical Settings of Nietzsche Texts: An Annotated Bibliography,' (I) *Nietzsche-Studien* 4 (1975), 284–323; (II) *Nietzsche-Studien* 5 (1976), 355–383; (III) *Nietzsche-Studien* 15 (1986), 440–452.
2. 'Scherz, List und Rache,' KSA 3, 356.

Or as he put in *The Case of Wagner*: '"Whatever is good, is easy; all that is divine treads nimbly": first principle of my aesthetics.'[1] Yet relatively few composers of songs tried their hands at that lighter material of Nietzsche. In the selection of music on the recordings accompanying this book, there is an emphasis on small-scale compositions, in which the light and dancing side of Nietzsche becomes more prominent. Moreover a number of the tracks are songs that set to music texts by Nietzsche; those by Frederick Delius and Kerry Woodward are here available for the first time.

I have already called attention to the connection between Nietzsche's creativity as a philosopher, writer, poet and composer. His earliest surviving works are poems; and the very last he wrote – and made a fair copy of when the madness had already clutched him, on 1 and 2 January 1889 – is the cycle *Dionysus-Dithyrambs*. That he wrote poems at an early age need not surprise: it was part of his cultural baggage; he learned to write them at school and applied those skills for occasions at home. But Nietzsche continued writing poetry throughout his life, and in doing so he developed a voice of his own. What is striking is that his considerable lyrical output, which manifestly results from an inner urge, never stands on its own, but is always connected with his philosophical work. In his poems Nietzsche could adopt yet another perspective, not as an undermining, but as an addition and enhancement of his philosophical positions. That is precisely why we often meet with the marginal and unsettling character of the jester in his poetry, who mocks other people's earnestness – but especially his own – and puts it in perspective. That is true also for another character whose voice is often heard in Nietzsche's poetry: the outsider, the loner, the tramp, the hermit, 'Prince Vogelfrei'. The cycles are often added to his philosophical works in the way of poetic comments: *Jest, Ruse and Revenge to The Gay Science* (1882), *Songs of Prince Vogelfrei* as an appendix to a later edition of that same work (1887); the many poetic passages in *Zarathustra*, where the boundaries between the various literary forms of expression become fluid; he wrote the *Dionysus Dithyrambs* in direct connection with his feverish last works, in which philosophy and autobiography merge and Nietzsche identifies himself ever more with the god Dionysus. It is with that name, too, that he signs *Ecce Homo:* '– Have I been understood? – *Dionysus against the Crucified...* [2] From that cycle several poems have been set to music by other composers, and in them, Nietzsche's favoured themes are prominent: life affirmation, loneliness, the gaining of power by overcoming resistance.

What is true for Nietzsche's compositions is even more so for his poetry: it is part of his comprehensive attempt to express the ineffable. The urgency that manifests itself in his philosophical work also searches its way out through all other available channels. It is this insistence that made and still continues to make Nietzsche appeal to artists. Undoubtedly, his choice of topics has an important part to play here, too: his emphasis on creativity and playfulness. But most of all, because Nietzsche was a dazzlingly versatile artist in his own philosophizing and, as it were, embodied the importance of art in the way he lived, he inspired

1. '"Das Gute ist leicht, alles Göttliche läuft auf zarten Füssen": erster Satz meiner Aesthetik.' *Der Fall Wagner* (KSA 6, 134).
2. '– Hat man mich verstanden? – *Dionysos gegen den Gekreuzigten...'* (KSA 6, 374).

and challenged so many others. This is where his greatness lies. This urgency also reveals itself in his best compositions.

And that is why Nietzsche wrote such good music.

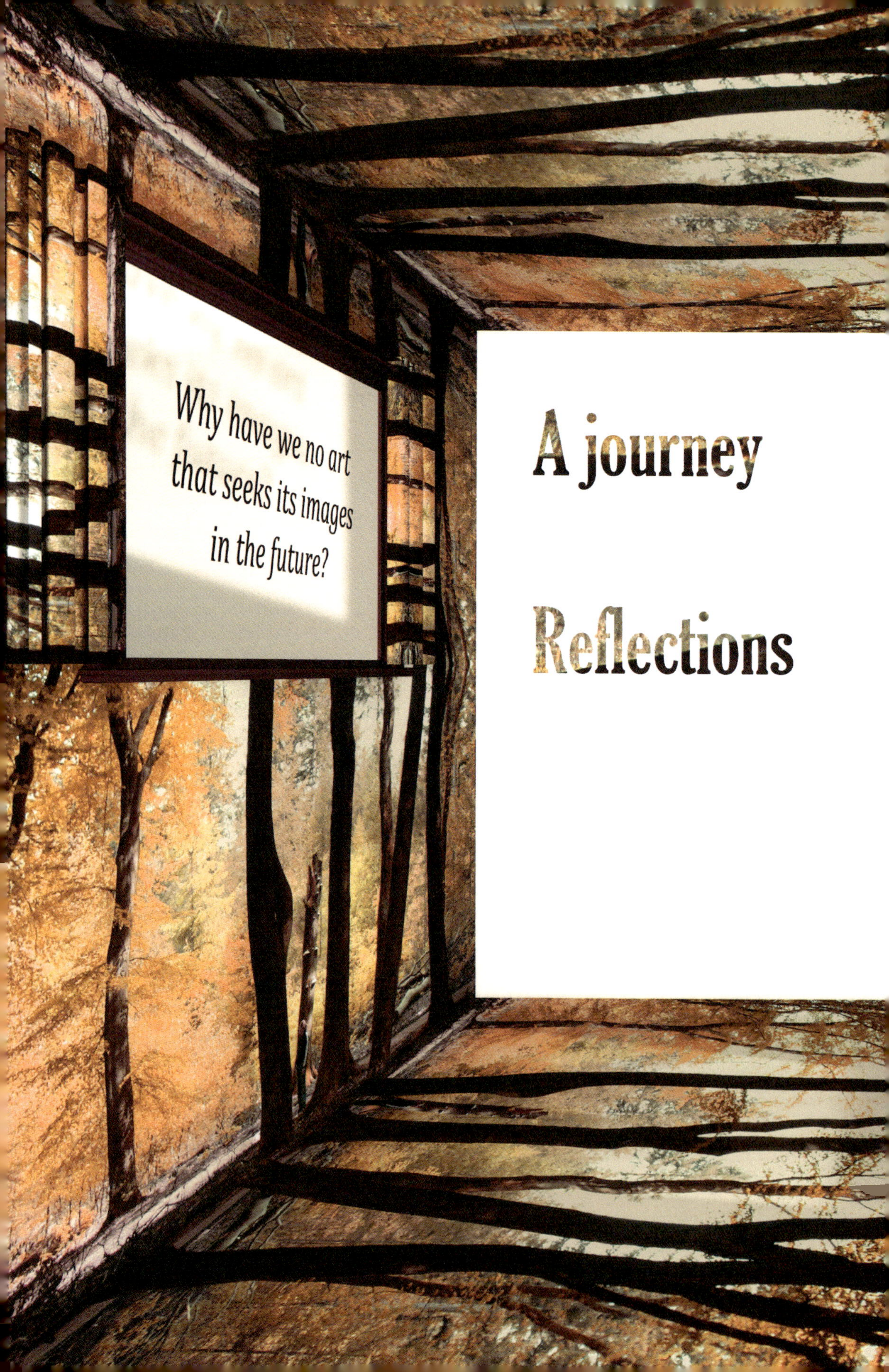

A journey

Reflections

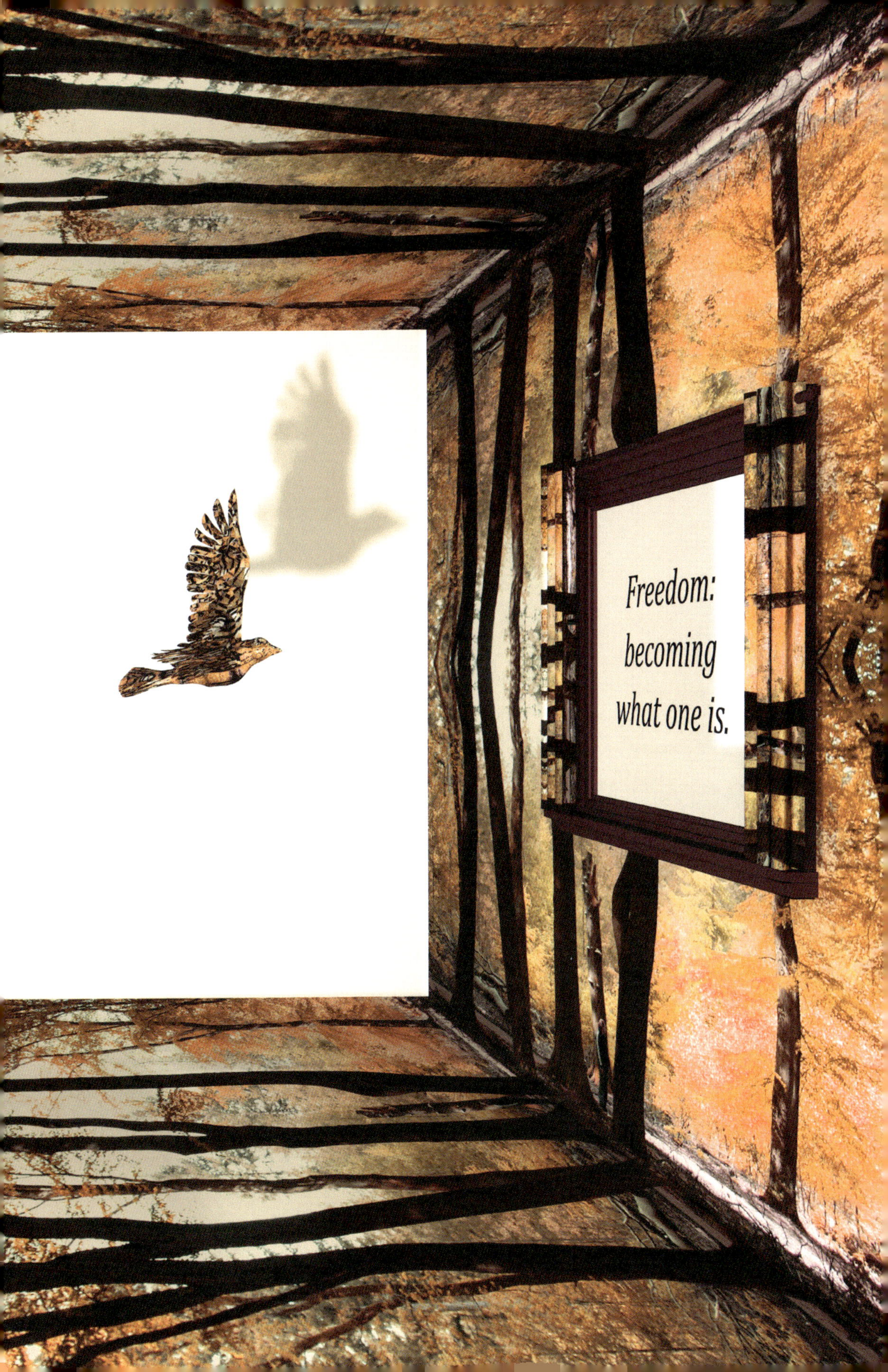
Freedom:
becoming
what one is.

A journey

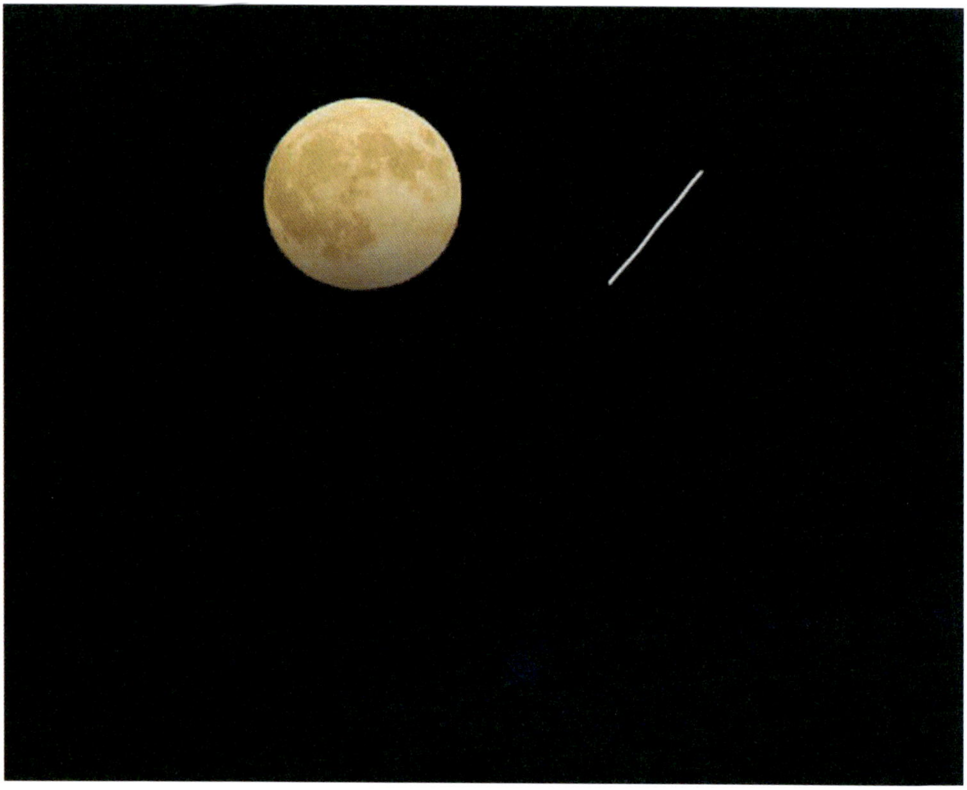

a-line-in-outer-space-1984 Martin Sjardijn

Under a low reddening sky **Martin Sjardijn** and I are looking for oysters on the coast of Zeeland to take to our hosts. Kerry and Anne Woodward invited us to cross the Channel and talk with them about Nietzsche's thoughts about the future of art and how art might 'seek its images in the future.' We pitch our tent, which shows a couple of holes in its roof, are amazed by the warm weather so early in spring, and trust that it won't rain. The next morning we drive on to France and make a stop at La Grand Fort Philippe. From the boulevard, the ocean seems not too far away, but soon we find that the beach is kilometres wide. We keep going as we tread with care on to the soil of cracked clay as if we might damage it. The waves are tempting.

At Rodin's monument 'Les Bourgeois de Calais' in front of the town hall, Martin asks me if I notice that the statues seem to be floating, as if tilted forward. God and Adam are floating without weight and, by this spiritual effect, the attention is drawn to the space around the sculpture. In the park, adorned with scenting flowers all around, I am given a lecture about the history of sculpture, starting with the flat, two-dimensional images of the Egyptians, then the three-dimensional statues of the early Greeks, like the 'Charioteer' (from the fifth century BC), and much later, the introduction of the 'contrapposto', whereby the hip is tilted and the weight shifted on to one foot.

Then the sixteenth century statues with extended bodies and limbs, which make them seem to float, as in the free anatomy of Michelangelo's 'Pietà'. The son, weightless, rests in the arms of the mourning mother. This weightlessness one also finds in the 'Christ on the Cross', seen as from above, by Saint John of the Cross in that same century. Suddenly Martin remarks that there are some interesting sites about 'weightless sculpture' on the internet, and mentions Wim Nijenhuis, an architect and philosopher who is just as eccentric as an architect as Martin claims to be as an artist.

He inspired me greatly, in 1991 Wim and I founded the 'Ubique', a think tank of artists who did research on the results, meaning and possibilities of the new electronic media, cyberspace and the new virtual reality.

The next morning, when we are boarding the ferry, I am trying to get Martin's attention for an interview and ask him if he always has been fascinated by space. He nods, opening his mouth, turns to the sea and sees a gannet. The binoculars are still in the car.

In Dover, we disembark and Martin seems to have no problem with driving on the left. The town, a target of heavy bombardments during the Second World War, is a major port in Kent on the Straits of Dover. Under a clear blue sky and, with its alluring modern architecture, nothing reminds us of those destructions.

We just manage to avoid colliding with an oncoming car, Martin forgot for a moment that oncoming traffic is on the right. After a lecture on the dangers of driving, he remembers how his father always kept a washcloth and some soap on the dashboard to give an impression of respectability and cleanliness. But with Martin's lengthy locks left in the barbershop long ago, customs' officers show not the least suspicion. We go through all barriers without even having to show passports once. I remember the Seventies when we were almost turned inside out before being allowed to set foot on this land; then, booze and cigarettes were found, now, with nothing to smuggle, nobody apprehends us.

Look out, look out… A lorry misses us by a hairsbreadth…
I decide to trust 'my' driver and surrender. Here, on the other side of the North Sea we see cat's claw, sand wheat, marram and flowers with yellow caps that I can't identify.

A pleasant sea breeze comes in through the open windows, its smell intoxicating. Never again do I want to go by plane, which gets you to your destination in no time, but where you never get to see all these narrow lanes with their banks full of flowers. I lean back watching the sun mirror the white cliffs of Dover on to the imposing castle walls with its fourth century roman lighthouse remains. After a second lecture on driving, I restart the interview.

'Your main passion seems to be weightlessness and virtual reality. Looking you up in the English Wikipedia, I see that you have been working on images in outer space for a long time.'

My work with immersion in interactive virtual reality was preceded by an idea I had in 1984. This was about a line in outer space, orbiting the earth at about three hundred kilometres, still visible with the naked eye. After a long period of painting, in which the work of Francis Bacon was an important source of inspiration, this idea started to haunt me. But in order to create something in outer space, you need technical knowledge and so I contacted Erik Jansen, professor of physics. He let me team up with one of his students who was doing a perception research with the aid of the, then hardly known, 'virtual reality' technique. I wondered if I could simulate weightlessness using these same techniques. That's how I was introduced to this new space that we call cyberspace these days. The computer was emerging fast, so in no time I was able to assemble programs and information from the internet.

The first idea for the 'Elements' installation, which I showed at the exhibition 'The Art of Nietzsche', originated with a pioneering virtual reality experiment at the Technical University of Delft, in 1991. It was concerned with the experiencing of an empty virtual universe: cyberspace. I looked at this void as a five-dimensional realm related to the void of the 'Black Square' of Malevich. In that virtual space I placed three three-dimensional fundamental objects: sphere, cube and cone, as a basic starting point for any creation in cyberspace. You can manipulate these basic elements using a Head Mounted Display and a Data Glove with tactile feedback.

> We take an attractive, alternative route that brings us to Anne and Kerry's, only three hours later than intended. On our left, the sea with its pebble beaches, behind us, the chalk cliffs with birds nestling on the rocks. We see gulls and a kittiwake.

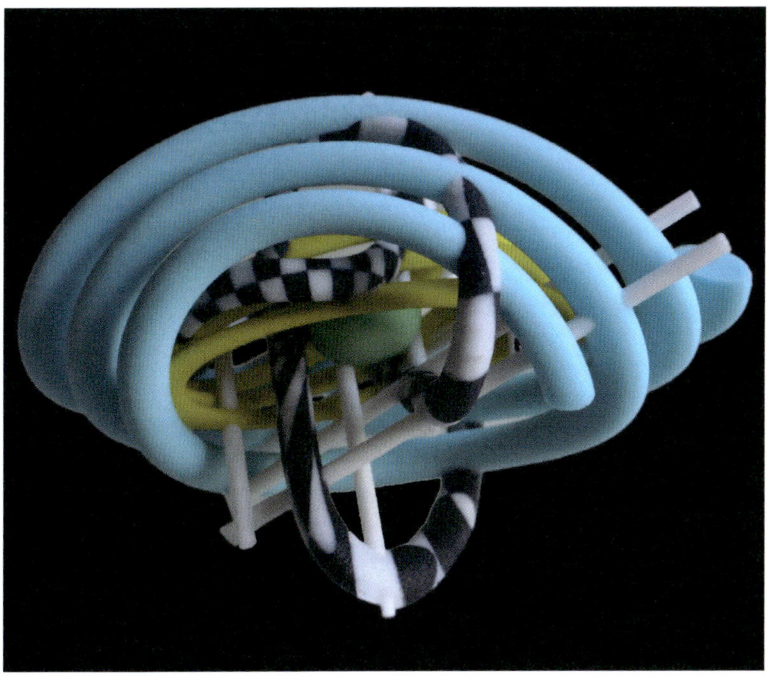

cyber - Martin Sjardijn

Listening with the ears of love

Anne and **Kerry Woodward** live some twenty minutes walk from the town. We take a shortcut, climbing over fences under a cacophony of finches, titmice, sparrows and other indefinable birds and finally arrive at the centre. Martin is expatiating on topics such as 'living in flocks', and 'look, that one is a solitaire', he can't stop explaining... Taking turns with his extendable binoculars, we search the chestnut trees and sycamores hoping for just a glance of other tiny birds, eager to mate. I'm beginning to differentiate between warblers, chiffchaff and nightingales, though more guesswork than knowledge.

Battle is a small town near the coast in East Sussex. Here, in 1066, the Battle of Hastings took place when William the Conqueror defeated the last of the Anglo-Saxon kings. The now famous Battle Abbey was built as penance for the victory. Nowadays there is a pleasant bustle of tourists queuing and enjoying themselves. One can only see friendly queues like this in England. I'm going to have an interview with Kerry somewhere here and he looks around for a place where we won't be distracted by too much noise.

Opposite the Abbey, amongst hoards of children with beautiful mothers who just seem to want to talk to each other, he finds an empty table.

'Kerry, what do you think of the quality of Nietzsche's music?'

He clears his throat and signals the waitress to put the coffees on our table. We are asked to pay for it immediately, but neither of us has any money. I forgot you can't use euros in England, and Kerry has no money with him, Anne normally carries it. 'There's a post office over there', the woman says patiently, pointing her chubby arm at a wall behind us. Kerry explains that we are waiting for friends who have money and will pay later. The waitress, at first wanting to stick to her rules, decides she can trust us. She gives us a friendly nod and returns to the bar where loaded trays are waiting to be served out. Leaning with one elbow on the table, Kerry says:

Nietzsche was constantly experimenting, trying out new things, then moving on to the next piece before finishing the first one. He wrote some liturgical music, his father was a preacher, and he had some difficulty overcoming that influence; also some parts of a Mass, interesting but quite frustrating for us, because, as I said, he hardly ever completed his compositions. His lack of technical skill probably made it problematic for him to work out the details. His best achievements were in shorter songs; these he usually completed. They're not intricate, actually rather simple. Some have pleasing melodies but certainly don't compare with the nineteenth century songs of composers like Schubert or Schumann.

'Nietzsche studied theology for a short while, graduated as a philologist and then concentrated on philosophy. When did he start to write music?'

He dreamed of being a composer, his first and greatest love was music. Then came philosophy, though again, he was more interested in experimenting than in teaching it. It was in his poetry that he found a way to express what he couldn't say in prose.

'How do you judge his poetry artistically and intellectually?'

Nietzsche sought various ways to express his thoughts and feelings. His poems, full of passion are, in my opinion, quite brilliant. Here he has the skills and is able to portray ideas that he might perhaps have wanted to put in his music. In his poetry one reads what is beyond words, fragments of thoughts but full of hidden meaning. Beautiful!

'It seems Nietzsche preferred music to words. He thought words always imply a separation from reality whereas "music is a direct expression of the will to power". In his music, did he allow himself be carried away by his feelings and his intuitions, by thunder and lightning?'

Yes, I'm certain he was driven by inspiration but that is not enough. A composer has to follow particular rules. Also, studying the techniques of the great composers might teach you how to write your own music. I don't suppose Nietzsche did that in any serious way.

'Did he set his own poems to music or did he write poems to fit his music?'

He never set his own poetry to music and it is quite rare for a poem to be written to fit the music. People who write musicals sometimes do it that way round, first the melody, then the lyrics. But composers generally don't, and neither did Nietzsche. Anyhow, he must have been rather a good pianist, for his piano compositions are sometimes quite virtuosic.

He started to write some orchestral pieces, not very accomplished, he didn't really know how all the different instruments worked. He knew enough about the piano and the violin to compose some rather good pieces for them, and that goes for a few piano duets as well.

We talk of Nietzsche's relationships and his friendship with Wagner, which had been so distorted by conflict and misunderstandings. From the corner of my eye I see Anne and Martin sitting at a nearby table. Good, the bill will be paid.

At the tables around us lunches are being served, mainly salads. Remembering the English food of the seventies, I momentarily long for fish and chips wrapped up in a Times or Daily Mirror. The inevitable association of licking ink from my pen comes up when I remember how the newspaper print pressed onto the fish.

'Did Nietzsche compose differently after he became ill than when he was younger? After all, he did live another eleven years.'

He wrote nothing during his final insanity, and his previous writings seem to show no deterioration whatsoever. The insanity must suddenly have overtaken him. Nothing in his music indicates mental illness. He simply stopped.

'And in his poetry?'

Not that I am aware of. I read nearly all his poems; they are clear and comprehensible. I am using that word because, although he moves through spaces and dimensions sometimes difficult to comprehend, I believe I can understand what he means.

'Does intuition play a role in Nietzsche's art?'

Well, in the poem, *Das eherne Schweigen* ('The brazen silence'), which I set for a speaker and four voices, Nietzsche tells that only when you listen with your heart, will you have any chance of understanding. First, he casts his fishing rod five times using his normal five senses, but catches not a single fish. Only at the sixth is he successful where the singers, having echoed each of his failed attempts, sing the final word... L O V E... and yes, I do believe in Love the way others might believe in God.

'Yes, you set some of his poetry to music, did you choose a particular style?'

Realising that my music would also function as a link to other composers' music, I used a somewhat different musical style for each of my six pieces. In the first poem, *Der Einsame* ('The lonely one'), Nietzsche says he hates ruling or following others or telling them what to do and only wants to hide and be alone with himself. In a style somewhat reminiscent of Schoenberg, it is set for speaker and piano, paradoxically, obeying strict atonal rules. The intention of the music is, firstly to show the domination of the purely rational that Nietzsche hated and from which he wanted to escape, and then, at the end, the rules are dissolved as he, as it were, becomes liberated in his aloneness.

'Then how did Nietzsche respond to the music of Johann Sebastian Bach, composer of precision and musical laws?'

Well, that is different. Nietzsche loved Bach. He recognised him as a master of freedom within the law. You might say that Schoenberg's atonal style was a system of rational thinking. Atonality is just one method I use and here is intended more as a gesture towards imprisoning Nietzsche, and then allowing him to escape.

The next song is for mezzo-soprano, violin, speaker and piano. In this poem, *Nur Narr! Nur Dichter!* ('Only fool! Only poet!') Nietzsche approaches his audience both as jester and as poet. This poem is astonishing. For this piece, placed in a garden at sunset, I adopt a more romantic style than in the first, a style closer to

Alban Berg who, like Nietzsche in this poem, often reflects natural events with human emotion.

'Alban Berg, atonality again?'

It is atonal, but has a strong, emotional expression. Maybe it's also the reason why people feel more attracted to Berg than to Schoenberg. You can recognize his fingerprints by a tonality that paradoxically seems to disturb an underlying atonality.

Then comes a piece for violin and piano duet, *Ein närrischer Dichter*. Hard to translate, it implies a joking but an also grumbling poet. There are three characters here, represented by a violin and two piano players. The violin is the poet disturbing us from his higher realms, the pianist playing the lower parts is the fool who disturbs us. The other pianist, playing on the middle and higher keys, is the 'common man' who wants just a normal, pleasurable life, hardly relating to anyone else in easy-going, jazz-like music. The fool enters, the violin breaks in and all chaos then breaks loose...

The next song is a setting of Nietzsche's poem, *Ecce homo* ('Behold the Man'), the infamous words of Pontius Pilate on delivering Christ, tortured and crowned with thorns, to the people of Jerusalem. Nietzsche says that man is, in reality, fire, burning and consuming himself in order to evolve. This fiery scherzo is for violin and coloratura soprano declaiming, 'Assuredly, I am a flame'.

In the last song, *Ewigkeit* ('Eternity'), for soprano, mezzo-soprano, tenor, bass-baritone, violin, speaker and piano four-hands, all participants come together in music of great variety and exuberance that has just a hint of the eternal composer, J.S. Bach. It suggests a concept of eternity wherein the universe will constantly be recurring in identical forms. Nietzsche himself would resurrect and continue his 'thought experiments', pleading for the *amor fati* - the love of what must be.

A young man in a khaki shirt appears at the next table. Two children run towards him and, judging by their identical red hair, they have to be his. Lifting them onto his shoulders makes them scream even louder and we must stop our conversation. Later, on my recording, I hear their echoes.

There's a twinkle in Kerry's eyes. And we laugh about the outer noise, I'm pretty sure of his project's success, especially now with this preview of its inner tone of...
L O V E

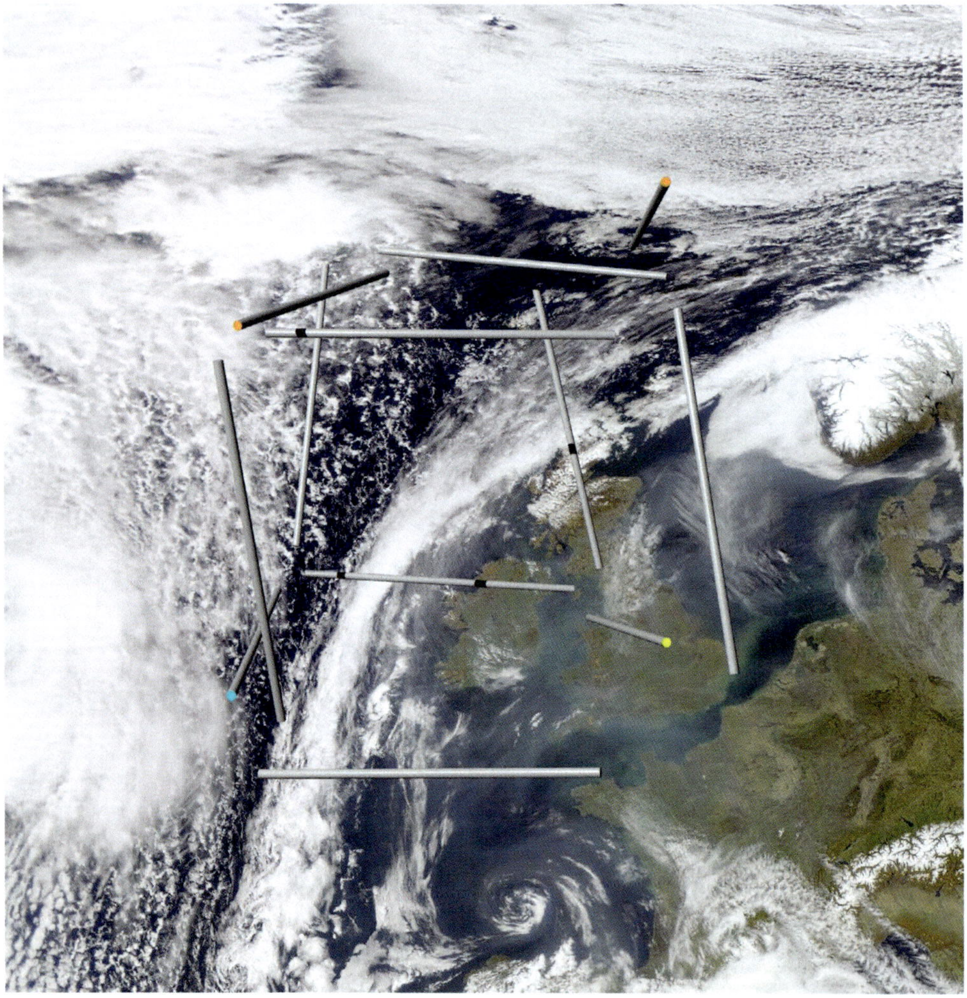

study-for-weightless-cube-1995 Martin Sjardijn

Return

Next morning we rise from the breakfast table and into our dented car, receive another dent in a confrontation with an old oak, turn left where we should have turned right, arriving at Dover harbour even earlier than we planned. For an extra ten pounds we can board immediately. Seagulls wheel alongside us. Suspended like airborne kites, they appear as making the crossing with not a single flap of their wings.

Again the weather is beautiful, but the wind keeps us inside.
Through the window we keep track of the 'kite' gulls and order some coffee. The floors, furniture and windows, everything on this boat is spick and span, the employees courteous. Unbeknown to Martin, I place my iPhone on the table and ask him about a subject that came up briefly yesterday.

'I heard you talking with Kerry about the possible future of science and art'

We discussed what art is supposed to be about, what it means now to be an artist. I am not interested in making art as such. Making art is imitation. It's impossible. Either it's there or not. Art should cross borders with no particular purpose and give openness, freedom. Art is purposeless, with only wonder at its core, and unrelated to all kinds of patterns and restrictions that should really be left behind. You can then enter the realm that one could call 'freedom', and this possibility of freedom, according to Kerry, is only in art. Not in philosophy, nor in technology. I am of a different opinion, however, and think technology is driven by art.

'Is that why the Technical University in Delft wants you to work with them?'

Yes, they opt for collaboration with artists because the attitude needed in scientific research is very similar to that of the 'true' artist, not of those who attempt to make art. What was seen as art in the past is now found in museums and is still being imitated by some young people under the illusion they are making art. But that is not so.

'Does that mean that all art has to be innovative?'

The trouble with Postmodernism was that it was confronted by the difficulty of making further innovation. Concepts like truth and romantic authenticity, cherished for so long, were called into question. But, in my opinion, innovation is not all that difficult so long as you maintain the urge to develop new things.

Martin is convinced that 'the earth is done', as he puts it. For the first time relaxed, he leans back, the wrinkle of concentration above his nose gone.

A few minutes later he starts grumbling about those 'contemporary architects who still focus on the material excesses of the twentieth century in order to sell their designs to countries who want to imitate the West'.

This is really reverse engineering. The West is superior in terms of technology. But, while things have been dramatically miniaturized since the arrival of the computer, they still create the large buildings we needed at the beginning of the twentieth century. An architect making buildings in Abu Dhabi even taller than those in New York is uninteresting. Money is their sole drive because, of course, the VIPs there love to outperform the West. I once told a group of architects that if I were an architect with the urge to erect buildings, I would build on the moon. When I started to venture from the arts into the extra-terrestrial space and cyberspace, I suddenly found myself in virgin spaces, spaces without history. Imagine touching something there... can you imagine?
What intrigues me most, is weightless motion, it's really special to work with that. You touch something... imagine a large cube that you can move simply by nudging it. That is all. Ask the people working with it at the university, you prod, it moves... you touch it with a fingertip, and there it goes once again...

The first time I found myself in the darkness of cyberspace, I kept seeking contact with the space outside. I was scared, afraid of the emptiness. Between the virtual reality glasses and my cheek I looked for something to hold on to. I wanted to feel my feet. I wanted to explain how it felt and said: if you do this - he covers his eyes with his hand - then everything ceases to be. Nothing but space, black space with innumerable stars. It's black, close your eyes and you'll see darkness... imagine the stars. Ultimate freedom...

I point at a breathless seagull, apparently wanting to travel with us. This man, usually too impatient to sit still for more than fifteen minutes, is now totally relaxed. We look out seeing the gulls, motionless and still hanging in the sky. It makes us laugh, and I wonder if he would like to be as free as these birds.

'Looking at your website, I also see traditional and figurative paintings of yours, some rather romantic. I can't quite reconcile that with everything you've just said.'

I don't have to throw the baby out with the bathwater. I'm standing on the shoulders of my forebears and do still need some backing and support. It's okay to look at one's mother once in a while. And the mother is romanticism and the history of art.

Under a clear blue sky we're sailing into Calais harbour. Tireless gulls circle around the recently docked fishing boats. I think I see a gannet among them. Just before the boat docks, they disappear. On the quay, new passengers wait, ready for the crossing.

Reflections

Back home, the crackling old transistor radio oozes some seventies music, 'Goldfinger, a spider's touch', 'but her heart was cold, she loves gold, only gold'... a voluptuous girl moaning in a bath of liquid gold, desirous of only one thing, wealth, imagining a gilded body as the pinnacle of pleasure. The girl dies, her skin shrivelled.

Wolfgang Rihm wrote a song cycle for baritone and piano and an opera based on Nietzsche's last work, the *Dionysus Dithyrambs*. According to some, these poems already show traces of insanity, but to others they are proof of his genius and crystal-clear insight into the nature of reality.

Nietzsche identified with Dionysos. In his autobiography, *Ecce homo*, he writes 'Dionysus' instead of his own name, several times. He believed it to be his lonely, Dionysian mission to change the world and, like Christ, not to bring peace, but the sword. Truths, certainties, all identities based on fixed principles must be destroyed in order for us to become what we truly are... a bridge to the Superman.

Composer Wolfgang Rihm, fascinated his whole life by Nietzsche's final works, described the essence of art as '*Ortlosigkeit*', placelessness, unrestricted by any place. Art has a Nietzschean mission: through art you can become dissociated from what, where and who you think you are.

Swirling his mallets, the timpanist summons thunder in Rihm's early opera, 'Dionysos'. We are seeing a performance of it at the Holland Festival in Amsterdam. After a long period working on our Nietzsche book, we're now tossed around in a bath of despair and agony. Nietzsche's sufferings, madness and oppression, so oppressive, apparently, that, after the interval, many chairs are now empty. We get carried away by the top E's of soprano 'Ariadne', by the violins taking over her notes flawlessly and by two nymphs taunting the principal character, N, who is incapable of reaching them.

One of them disappears into the fog, the other is transformed into Ariadne, willing to surrender, and even to be tied down by him if he would only just say something. Finally, with great effort N utters the few words: 'I... am... your... labyrinth'. With those same words, spoken with conviction, N's friend, 'ein Gast', is able to conquer Ariadne with ease. Wherever he goes, N always is confronted with loneliness. Rivals at first, N now tries climbing to the top of a mountain with 'ein Gast'. A thunderstorm threatens to hurl them both into a ravine, but the higher they climb, the lighter N begins to feel. Proximity both to heaven and death shifts him into a state of bliss. Though he still continues searching for love, N increasingly imprisons himself in his own world of images. Then Apollo appears, reason opposing delight, and skins him. His flayed skin starts to move by itself and all turn away from N in horror. We remember Suzanne Bo's fascination with skin, which she uses to show both the boundary between the individual and the world, and between the outer and inner beings of man.

N's skin witnesses a horse being beaten by a faceless man. Is it 'ein Gast'? Is it Apollo? The skin wants to embrace the horse and collapses into the arms of Ariadne. N has found his truth. A flash of lightning and then, in emerald green splendour, Dionysos reappears. To live the Dionysian way, do we have to sacrifice our skin and open ourselves to ultimate vulnerability? Do we have to leap into insanity?

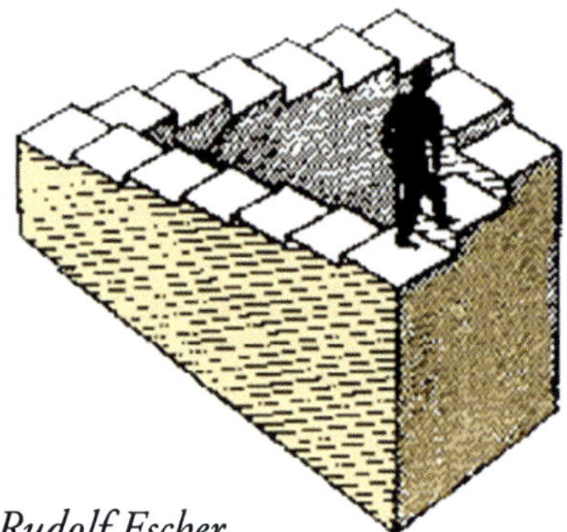

Rudolf Escher

By positing an eternal recurrence of all things, Nietzsche chooses to use a spatial metaphor of the closed line or circuit, or rather a variation thereof that concerns the passing of time. We might imagine the Superman as ascending the steps and the 'herd man' going the other way, always descending. Does this optical illusion illustrate a mental one?

Nietzsche's god is dead and Zarathustra is presented as a prophet of the eternal recurrence. The hermit finally discovers that a hermit is nothing but an individual focused on himself, so much so, that he is all the time conscious of two personalities within. 'Me and myself talk to each other too furiously'. So, finally, the hermit needs a friend desperately, to keep himself from drowning. Zarathustra concludes that we need a friend to satisfy an inner desire, the desire to climb higher. This need for friendship or love displays our fragility.

Does an artist search for unknown altitudes, for the sublime in his creation? Is he the solitary individual, 'furiously conversing' with his alter ego, and, like Zarathustra, searching for the friend who could keep him afloat? And is he also the driving force behind science and new technical developments?

Are you living your life in such a way that you would want to relive it for all eternity? Is it 'true' that only he who answers 'yes' to this question has liberated himself? Or can we be free through understanding, freed from insecurity and pain because we know that it passes and will turn into something positive?

No final conclusions can be drawn from our attempts to look at Nietzsche from the perspective of the artist. That would be completely against his spirit and in contradiction with the fluidity of his truth. But, by listening to composers such as Mahler, Orff, Webern, Rihm and Woodward, who have understood who Nietzsche the poet was and, by looking at artworks, pondering the future of art, we might get a glimpse of the freedom and confirmation of life that Nietzsche so passionately yearned for.

The Music

1. **Das Wort** - speaker
2. **Der Einsame**, *Kerry Woodward* – speaker and piano[2]
3. **Der Einsame**, *Frederick Delius* - soprano and piano[2]
4. **Nur Narr! Nur Dichter!** *Kerry Woodward* - mezzo-soprano, violin, speaker and piano[2]
5. **Narr und Dichter**, *Kerry Woodward* - violin and piano duet
6. **Der Wandrer**, *Frederick Delius* - tenor and piano[2]
7. **Der Wandrer und sein Schatten**, *Frederick Delius* - bass-baritone and piano[2]
8. **Mazurka**, *Friedrich Nietzsche* - piano[1]
9. **Das zerbrochene Ringlein**, *Friedrich Nietzsche* (Eichendorff) – speaker and piano[1]
10. **Heiter**, *Anton Webern* - mezzo-soprano and piano[1]
11. **Mein Herz ist wie ein See so weit**, *Carl Orff* - soprano en piano[1]
12. **O weint um sie!**, *Friedrich Nietzsche* (Byron) - soprano, mezzo- soprano,tenor, bass-baritone and piano[1]
13. **Herbstlich sonnige Tage**, *Friedrich Nietzsche* (Geibel) - soprano, mezzo-soprano, tenor, bass-baritone
14. **Eine Sylvesternacht**, *Friedrich Nietzsche* - violin and piano[1]
15. **Gebet an das Leben**, *Friedrich Nietzsche* (Salomé) - soprano and piano[1]
16. **Der Einsamste**, *Wolfgang Rihm* - bass-baritone and piano[1]
17. **Der Wandrer**, *Wolfgang Rihm* - bass-baritone and piano[1]
18. **Das eherne Schweigen**, *Kerry Woodward* - speaker, soprano, mezzo-soprano, tenor, bass-baritone
19. **Ecce Homo**, *Kerry Woodward* - soprano en violin
20. **Nach neuen Meeren**, *Frederick Delius* - tenor and piano[1]
21. **Noch ein Mal**, *Frederick Delius* - bass-baritone and piano[1]
22. **Zarathustra's Mitternachtslied**, *Gustav Mahler* - mezzo-soprano, violin and piano[1]
23. **Ewigkeit**, *Kerry Woodward* - soprano, mezzo-soprano, tenor, bass-baritone, violin, speaker and piano duet

All the song texts are by Friedrich Nietzsche, except those he used in his own compositions.

Website: http://transmusings.org/home/The_Art_of_Nietzsche_Music.html

Musicians:

Claudia Patacca - soprano, **Janneke Schaareman** - mezzo-soprano, **Falco van Loon** - tenor, **Vincent Spoeltman** - bass-baritone, **Justyna Briefjes** - violin, **Meinard Kraak** - speaker, **Simon Marlow**[1], **Jacob Engel**[2] - piano

Recording Engineer - **Paul-Peter Polak**

1. Das Wort

Lebend'gem Worte bin ich gut:
Das springt heran so wohlgemuth,
Das grüßt mit artigem Genick,
Ist lieblich selbst im Ungeschick.
Hat Blut in sich, kann herzhaft schnauben,
Kriecht dann zum Ohre selbst den Tauben
Und ringelt sich und flattert jetzt
Und was es tut - das Wort ergetzt.
Doch bleibt das Wort ein zartes Wesen,
Bald krank und aber bald genesen.
Willst ihm sein kleines Leben lassen,
Mußt du es leicht und zierlich fassen,
Nicht plump betasten und bedrücken,
Es stirbt oft schon an bösen Blicken -
Und liegt dann da, so ungestalt,
So seelenlos, so arm und kalt,
Sein kleiner Leichnam arg verwandelt,
Von Tod und Sterben mißgehandelt.
Ein totes Wort - ein häßlich Ding,
Ein klapperdürres Kling-Kling-Kling.
Pfui allen häßlichen Gewerben,
An denen Wort und Wörtchen sterben!

2. Der Einsame

Verhasst ist mir das Folgen und das Führen.
Gehorchen? Nein! Und aber nein – Regieren!
Wer sich nicht schrecklich ist, macht Niemand Schrecken:
Und nur wer Schrecken macht, kann Andre führen.
Verhasst ist mir's schon, selber mich zu führen!
Ich liebe es, gleich Wald- und Meeresthieren,
Mich für ein gutes Weilchen zu verlieren,
In holder Irrniss grüblerisch zu hocken,
Von ferne her mich endlich heimzulocken,
Mich selber zu mir selber — zu verführen.

1. The word

The living word is my companion:
Who jumps up at me so cheerfully,
And greets me with a friendly nod,
Lovely even in its awkwardness,
Full-blooded, snorting heartily,
Even crawling into deaf ears,
Entwining itself and now fluttering,
And whatever it does - the word delights.
Even so, the word remains a tender being,
Soon sick, though quickly cured.
To let it have its little life,
Hold it light and delicate,
Don't touch or squeeze it roughly,
Often it will die just from evil glances –
And lies there then, so deformed,
So soulless, poor and cold,
Its tiny corpse wickedly transformed,
Abused by death and dying.
A dead word – a hideous thing,
A bone-dry rattling kling-kling-kling.
Yuck to all those hateful trades,
Wherein word and words expire!

2. The lonely one

I loathe following and leading.
Obeying? No! And again no – to governing!
Whoever does not terrify himself, cannot terrify others:
And only one who terrifies, can lead others!
I even hate leading myself!
What I love, like creatures of the sea and forest,
Is to lose myself for a good little while,
To crouch pensively in sweet error,
From far away to lure myself finally home,
To seduce myself - to myself.

3. Der Einsame (as no. 2)

4. Nur Narr! Nur Dichter!

Bei abgehellter Luft,
Wenn schon des Monds Sichel
Grün zwischen Purpurröthen
Und neidisch hinschleicht:
— dem Tage feind,
Mit jedem Schritte heimlich
An Rosen-Hängematten
Hinsichelnd, bis sie sinken,
Nacht-abwärts blass hinabsinken: —

So sank ich selber einstmals
Aus meinem Wahrheits-Wahnsinne,
Aus meinen Tages-Sehnsüchten,
Des Tages müde, krank vom Lichte,
— sank abwärts, abendwärts, schattenwärts:
Von Einer Wahrheit
Verbrannt und durstig:
— gedenkst du noch, gedenkst du, heisses Herz,
Wie da du durstetest? —
Dass ich verbannt sei
Von aller Wahrheit,
Nur Narr!
Nur Dichter!

5. Narr und Dichter

6. Der Wandrer

„Kein Pfad mehr! Abgrund rings und Todtenstille!“ —
So wolltest du’s! Vom Pfade wich dein Wille!
Nun, Wandrer, gilt’s! Nun blicke kalt und klar!
Verloren bist du, glaubst du — an Gefahr.

3. The lonely one (as no.2)

4. Only fool! Only poet!

In a darkening sky,
When the crescent moon
Green amongst purple
Is already creeping down, enviously:
- enemy to the day,
With every furtive step
Crescents down the hanging rose-gardens
Until, pale, they sink
Down towards the night: -

So I myself once sank
From my madness for truth,
From my daytime aspirations,
Weary of day, sick with light
- sank downwards, evening-wards, shadow-wards,
With one truth
Scorched and thirsty
- are you still mindful, are you, hot heart,
Of how you thirsted then? –
Let me be banished
From all truth!
Only fool!
Only poet!

5. Fool and Poet

6. The wanderer

"No path left! Encircled by precipice and deathly silence!" -
You wanted it! Your will strayed from the path!
Now, wanderer, this is it! Look now cold and clear!
You are lost, if you think - about danger.

7. Der Wanderer und sein Schatten

Nicht mehr zurück? Und nicht hinan?
Auch für die Gemse keine Bahn?

So wart' ich hier und f a s s e fest
Was Aug' und Hand mich fassen läßt!

Fünf Fuß breit Erde, Morgenroth,
Und u n t e r mir – Welt, Mensch und Tod!

8. Mazurka

9. Das zerbrochene Ringlein

In einem kühlen Grunde
Da geht ein Mühlenrad,
Meine Liebste ist verschwunden,
Die dort gewohnet hat.

Sie hat mir Treu' versprochen,
Gab mir ein'n Ring dabei,
Sie hat die Treu' gebrochen,
Das Ringlein sprang entzwei.

Ich möcht' als Spielmann reisen
Wohl in die Welt hinaus,
Und singen meine Weisen,
Und gehn von Haus zu Haus.

Ich möcht als Reiter fliegen
Wohl in die blut'ge Schlacht,
Um stille Feuer liegen
Im Feld bei dunkler Nacht.

Hör ich das Mühlrad gehen:
Ich weiss nicht, was ich will -
Ich möcht am liebsten sterben,
Da wär's auf einmal still! (Eichendorff)

7. The wanderer and his shadow

No way back? No way up?
No track even for a goat ?

Then I'll wait here and *cling* on to
Anything that eye and hand can hold!

Five feet across the earth, the dawn,
and *below* me – the world, man and death!

8. Mazurka

9. The broken ringlet

Down in the cold valley,
A millwheel turns.
My sweetheart has gone,
She used to live there.

She promised to be true to me,
Gave me a ring as well,
That promise she has broken,
My ringlet split in two.

I'd like to go as a minstrel
Out into the wide world,
And sing my airs,
Going from house to house.

I'd like to race as a cavalier
Into a real bloody battle,
Rest round a quiet fire
In a field at the dark of night.

I hear the millwheel going:
I don't know, what I want -
I'd like it best to die,
Then at once, all would be still.

10. Heiter

Mein Herz ist wie ein See so weit,
Drin lacht dein Antlitz Sonnenlicht
In tiefer süßer Einsamkeit,
Wo leise Well' an Well' sich bricht.

Ist's Nacht, ist's Tag?
Ich weiß es nicht,
Lacht doch auf mich so lieb und lind
Dein sonnenlichtes Angesicht
Und selig bin ich wie ein Kind.

11. Mein Herz ist wie ein See so weit (as no.10)

12. O weint um sie

O weint um sie, die einst an Babels Strand
Geweint, - ihr Tempel wüst, ein Traum ihr Land !
Weint um die Harfe Juda's, die zersprang, -
Abgötter sind, wo einst ihr Gott sich schwang.
(Byron. Translation: Adolf Böttger)

10. Serenity

My heart is vast as a lake,
Wherein your countenance is laughing sunlight
In deep, sweet solitude
With wave upon wave gently breaking.

Is it night, is it day?
I do not know,
but it smiles at me so sweet and gentle
your face of sunlight,
And I am happy as a child.

11. My heart is vast as a lake (as no.10)

12. Oh! weep for those

Oh! weep for those that wept by Babel's stream,
Whose shrines are desolate, whose land a dream;
Weep for the harp of Judah's broken shell;
Mourn - where their God that dwelt the godless dwell!

13. Herbstlich sonnige Tage

Herbstlich sonnige Tage,
Mir beschieden zur Lust,
Euch mit leiserem Schlage
Grüßt die atmende Brust.

O wie waltet die Stunde
Nun in seliger Ruh'!
Jede schmerzende Wunde
Schließet leise sich zu.

Nur zu rasten, zu lieben,
Still an sich selber zu baun
Fühlt sich die Seele getrieben
Und mit Liebe zu schaun.

Und so schreit' ich im Tale,
In den Bergen, am Bach
Jedem segnenden Strahle,
Jedem verzehrenden nach.

Jedem leisen Verfärben
Lausch' ich mit stillem Bemühn,
Jedem Wachsen und Sterben,
Jedem Welken und Blühn.

Selig lern' ich es spüren,
Wie die Schöpfung entlang
Geist und Welt sich berühren
Zu harmonischem Klang. (Emanuel Geibel)

14. Eine Sylvesternacht

13. Autumn's sunny days

Autumn's sunny days,
Given to me to enjoy,
My breathing breast greets
You with a softer heartbeat.

O how time basks
In blissful repose now!
Each painful wound
Is gently closing itself up.

Just to rest, to love,
To build quietly on itself,
So does the soul feel driven
To gaze with love.

And treading through the valley,
In the mountains, by the stream,
I follow those blissful rays
That consume everything.

I listen with silent attention
To all soft changes in colour,
To all that is growing and dying,
All things withering and blooming.

I blissfully learn to perceive
How, through the whole of creation,
Spirit and world touch each other
In harmonious sonority.

14. A New Year's Eve

15. Gebet an das Leben

Gewiß, so liebt ein Freund den Freund
wie ich dich liebe, rätselvolles Leben!
Ob ich in dir gejauchzt, geweint,
ob du mir Leid, ob du mir Lust gegeben,
ich liebe dich mit deinem Glück und Harme,
und wenn du mich vernichten mußt,
entreiße ich schmerzvoll mich deinem Arme,
gleich wie der Freund der Freundesbrust.

16. Der Einsamste

Nun, da der Tag
Des Tages müde ward, und aller Sehnsucht Bäche
Von Neuem Trost plätschern,
auch alle Himmel, aufgehängt in Gold-Spinnetzen,
zu jedem Müden sprechen: "ruhe nun", —
was ruhst du nicht, du dunkles Herz,
was stachelt dich zu fußwunder Flucht

weß harrest du?

15. Prayer to life

For certain, just as a friend loves a friend
So do I love you, O life enigmatic!
Whether I delight in you, or weep,
Whether you bring me sorrow or joy,
I love both your happiness and grief,
And if you must annihilate me,
I have to painfully tear myself from your arms,
Just as a friend would from the heart of a friend.

16. The loneliest one

Now, since the day
grown wearied from the day, and all yearning streams
are babbling with solace anew,
as indeed the sky, hung with gold-spun nets,
say to each weary soul: “now rest”, —
why do you not rest, dark heart,
what spurs you to wondrous flights of fancy

what are you expecting?

17. Der Wanderer

Es geht ein Wandrer durch die Nacht
Mit gutem Schritt;
Und krummes Thal und lange Höhn –
Er nimmt sie mit.
Die Nacht ist schön —
Er schreitet zu und steht nicht still,
Weiß nicht, wohin sein Weg noch will.

Da singt ein Vogel durch die Nacht:
"Ach Vogel, was hast du gemacht?
Was hemmst du meinen Sinn und Fuß
Und gießest süßen Herz-Verdruß
In's Ohr mir, daß ich stehen muß
Und lauschen muß – –
Was l o c k s t du mich mit Ton und Gruß?" —

Der gute Vogel schweigt und spricht:
"Nein Wandrer, nein! Dich lock' ich nicht
Mit dem Getön –
Ein Weibchen lock' ich von den Höhn
Was geht's dich an?
Allein ist mir die Nacht nicht schön.
Was geht's dich an? Denn du sollst gehn
Und nimmer, nimmer stille stehn!
Was stehst du noch?
Was tat mein Flötenlied dir an,
Du Wandersmann?"

Der gute Vogel schwieg und sann:
"Was tat mein Flötenlied ihm an?
Was steht er noch?
Der arme, arme Wandersmann!"

17. The wanderer

There goes a wanderer through the night
With resolute step;
Both winding valleys and high hills
He takes in his stride.
The night is lovely –
He marches on and never rests,
Not knowing where his path will go.

There sings a bird through the night:
"Ah, bird, what are you doing?
Why do you hinder my mind and foot
And pour sweet irritations of the heart
Into my ear, so that I have to stand
And listen – –
Why do you *lure* me with sound and greeting?" –

The good bird falls silent and says:
"No, wanderer, no! I'm not luring you
With my sounds –
I'm luring a little mate in the hills,
So what's that to you?
All alone, the night is not beautiful to me.
And what's that to you? Because you should walk
And never again keep still!
Why are you still standing there?
What has my flute-like song done to you,
You wandering man?"

The good bird fell silent and pondered:
"What has my flute-like song done to him?
Why is he still standing there?
The poor, poor wandering man!"

18. Das eherne Shweigen

Fünf Ohren – und kein Ton darin!
Die Welt ward stumm…

Ich horchte mit den Ohren meiner N e u g i e r d e
Fünf Mal warf ich die Angel über mich,
Fünf Mal zog ich keinen Fisch herauf –
Ich fragte – keine Antwort lief mir ins Netz –

Ich horchte mit dem Ohr meiner L I E B E .

19. Ecce homo

Ja! Ich weiss, woher ich stamme!
Ungesättigt gleich der Flamme
Glühe und verzehr' ich mich.
Licht wird Alles, was ich fasse,
Kohle Alles, was ich lasse:
Flamme bin ich sicherlich!

20. Nach neuen Meeren

Dorthin — w i l l ich; und ich traue
Mir fortan und meinem Griff.
Offen liegt das Meer, in's Blaue
Treibt mein Genueser Schiff.

Alles glänzt mir neu und neuer,
Mittag schläft auf Raum und Zeit —:
Nur d e i n Auge — ungeheuer
Blickt mich's an, Unendlichkeit!

18. The bronze silence

Five ears – and no sound therein!
The world became silent…

I listened with the ears of my *curiosity*
Five times I cast my rod,
Five times I pulled out no fish–
I asked – no answer came into my net –

I listened with the ear of my L O V E

19. Ecce Homo

Yes! I know from whence I come,
Insatiable as the flame
I glow and consume myself.
Everything I grasp becomes light,
Whatever I leave is ashes:
For, assuredly, I am flame!

20. Towards new oceans

Thither – I *will* go; and henceforth I trust
Myself and my grasp.
The ocean is open, into the blue
My Genoese sail is driven.

Everything glitters fresh and new,
Midday slumbers upon space and time
Only *your* eye – tremendous
Looks on me, boundlessness!

21. Noch ein Mal

Oh Mensch! Gieb Acht!
Was spricht die tiefe Mitternacht?
“Ich schlief, ich schlief —,
Aus tiefem Traum bin ich erwacht: —
Die Welt ist tief,
Und tiefer als der Tag gedacht.
Tief ist ihr Weh —,
Lust — tiefer noch als Herzeleid:
Weh spricht: Vergeh!
Doch alle Lust will Ewigkeit —,
— will tiefe, tiefe Ewigkeit!”

22. Zarathustra’s Mitternachtslied (as no. 21)

21. Yet once again

O man, take heed!
What says deep midnight?
"I slept, I slept —,
From deep dreams I have awoken: —
The world is deep,
And deeper than the day had thought.
Deep is its sorrow —,
Joy — deeper still than grief:
Sorrow says: Perish!
But joys all want eternity —,
— want deep, deep eternity!"

22. Zarathustra's Midnight Song (as no.21)

23. Ewigkeit

Höchstes Gestirn des Seins!
Ewiger Bildwerke Tafel!
Du kommst zu mir? —
Was Keiner erschaut hat,
deine stumme Schönheit, —
wie? sie flieht vor meinen Blicken nicht?

Schild der Nothwendigkeit!
Ewiger Bildwerke Tafel!
— aber du weisst es ja:
was Alle hassen,
was allein ich liebe,
dass du e w i g bist!
dass du n o t h w e n d i g bist!
Meine Liebe entzündet
sich ewig nur an der Nothwendigkeit.

Schild der Nothwendigkeit!
Höchstes Gestirn des Seins!
— das kein Wunsch erreicht,
das kein Nein befleckt,
ewiges Ja des Sein's,
ewig bin ich dein Ja:
d e n n i c h l i e b e d i c h, o h E w i g k e i t ! ——

23. Eternity

Supreme star of being!
Perpetual tablet of forms!
You come to me? —
That which none has beheld,
your muted loveliness, —
how? she flees not from my gaze?

Image of what must be!
Perpetual tablet of forms!
— But you know it well:
what all hate,
what I alone love,
that you are *eternal!*
that you are *necessary!*
My love is ignited
only by that which has to be.

Image of what must be!
Supreme star of being!
— That no desire can reach,
That no 'No' can taint,
Eternal Yes of being,
I am your eternal Yes:
Because I love you, o eternity! ——

13096191R00061

Printed in Great Britain
by Amazon.co.uk, Ltd.,
Marston Gate.